THE PERILS OF ACCENTUATING THE POSITIVE

Edited by
Robert B. Kaiser
Kaplan DeVries Inc.

HOGANPRESS

2622 E 21st Street Tulsa, OK 74114
www.hoganpress.com

ISBN 978-0-9816457-5-9

Dedication

For Claire and Ben. May you continue to learn and grow, not just in these early years, but forever.

RBK

Contents

Acknowledgments

This book is a collective accomplishment. Many of the authors, experts whose ideas I studied closely when cutting my professional teeth, helped create the modern field of management development. It is humbling to edit and compile the work of such accomplished figures. Each chapter is based on a mountain of practical experiences and scholarly achievements. From these peaks, the authors speak collectively with wisdom and authority.

This project began in the spring of 2007 as a session at the 22nd annual conference of the Society for Industrial and Organizational Psychology in New York City. The session featured Morgan McCall, Bob Kaplan, Bob Hogan, Mike Benson, and me speaking about "the perils of the positives." The presentations were well-received, so we decided to each write a brief chapter and bundle them in a short publication. As word got out that we were doing a project to call attention to the hidden dangers in the "strengths movement," more people expressed interest in contributing. The timing was right; it turns out that many seasoned and savvy experts have been growing concerned with the faddish, widespread adoption of the "strengths, strengths, strengths—all you need are strengths" mantra. The idea of cautionary guidance for those in the trenches interested in the strengths-based approach struck a chord. As a result, we offer this collected volume.

I am grateful to my colleagues for contributing their ideas, for their willingness to make connections between their own original thinking and the thinking expressed in other chapters, for their tolerance of a "hands-on" editor (to put it charitably), and for their commitment to the responsible practice of management development. Thank you, Bob Eichinger, Guangrong Dai, KingYii "Lulu" Tang, Jean Leslie, Anand Chandrasekar, Morgan McCall, Bob Kaplan, Steve Berglas, Bill Gentry, Craig Chappelow, Bob Hogan, Mike Benson, Mal Davies, and Randy White.

I owe an additional debt of gratitude to my mentor, colleague, and friend, Bob Kaplan. Bob was at the Center for Creative Leadership in the early 1980s when it was setting the standard for innovative research on management development. Imagine how rich it would have been to be a fly on the wall when Bob, Morgan McCall, Mike Lombardo, Ann Morrison, Randy White, Ellen Van Velsor, David DeVries, and their colleagues were making break-set discoveries about the lessons of experience, why successful managers derail, the glass ceiling, and what makes an executive tick. Morgan McCall and Mike Lombardo deserve credit for popularizing the phrase, "strengths can become weaknesses," but they were not the only ones to explore the topic.

In his characteristically incisive and independent way, Bob was off making his own discoveries about strengths overused in intense and deeply personal developmental work with individual executives. If Morgan and Mike cast a mile-wide net to discover the dynamics of derailment and found that strengths become weaknesses, then Bob drilled down a mile deep to discover the dynamics that drove individuals to get carried away with their strengths. His case study of "Rich Bauer" in *Beyond Ambition* (Jossey-Bass, 1991) is a penetrating and instructive analysis of how and why a strength can become a weakness. Bob also recognized that typical 360-degree surveys and their "more is better" 1-to-5 rating scales were not equipped to identify when strengths are overused, prompting him to work out a clever way to correct this design flaw. And in helping executives grow and improve, Bob also hit upon the novel insight that getting them to truly appreciate their strengths is both difficult and the necessary prior step to helping them make better use of their strengths. I continue to recommend his brief report, *Internalizing Strengths* (Center for Creative Leadership, 1999), to executives and development professionals alike.

I have been fortunate to join Bob in fleshing out and building solutions for applying his original insights since 1997. Without Bob's influence, I might never have taken such an interest in strengths-based development, nor would I have come to appreciate the many subtle nuances in the role strengths play in development. Thank you, Bob, for the inspiration, education, and opportunity.

Denise Craig deserves mention for her careful attention to detail in copyediting the final book manuscript. Alas, any errors, oversights, or inconsistencies are entirely mine. Jon Joyce gets credit for the design of the cover and appealing layout of the book.

Finally, I thank Hogan Assessment Systems and the Center for Creative Leadership, both trendsetters and role models of responsible practice in the assessment and development of managers, for providing this forum where thought leaders can offer their collective wisdom for those drawn to positive psychology and strengths-based development.

Rob Kaiser

Greensboro, NC

October 2008

About the Authors

Michael J. Benson is a Manager of Leadership Assessment and Development at Johnson & Johnson, based in New Brunswick, NJ. He previously worked for Personnel Decisions International and spent 12 years serving his country as an officer in the United States Air Force. He has numerous publications and presentations to his credit; the majority focus on leadership, development, and organizational performance. Mike has delivered leadership training sessions, performance feedback, and talent management consulting to military and corporate audiences. His genuine interest in partnering with individuals and organizations coupled with his balance of research-based knowledge and applied leadership experiences help him propel individuals and organizations to new heights. Mike has a Ph.D. in Industrial/Organizational Psychology from the University of Minnesota.

Steven Berglas is on the faculty of the UCLA Anderson School of Management. Previously, he was on the faculty of Harvard Medical School's Department of Psychiatry where he studied, and had a clinical practice devoted to, individuals with narcissistic personality disorders and/or self-defeating tendencies. Berglas authored (or coauthored) four books and over 60 publications on "the stress of success." Steve's coaching and consulting practice is devoted to super-successful individuals and organizations at risk for success-induced difficulties. Berglas received his B.A. from Clark University, his Ph.D. from Duke University, and did his postdoctoral training in psychiatry at Harvard Medical School.

Anand Chandrasekar is a research associate with the Center for Creative Leadership, and based at CCL's Asia campus in Singapore. His current research is focused on the leadership gap in organizations. Additionally, he has publications on cultural intelligence, expatriate adjustment, job burnout and has taught organizational behavior and human resource costing courses. Anand holds an M.Bus. in Organizational Behavior from Nanyang Technological University, Singapore.

Craig T. Chappelow is a senior faculty member at the Center for Creative Leadership. He manages CCL's retail 360-degree assessment business and is a lead trainer in a number of CCL's leadership programs. Craig recently coauthored the book *Leveraging the Impact of 360-Degree Feedback* (Pfeiffer, 2008). He has published articles in a wide variety of sources from the *Harvard Business Review* to *Southern Living*. Craig holds a bachelor's degree from MacMurray College and a master's degree from the University of Vermont.

Guangrong Dai joined the research team at Lominger International–A Korn/Ferry Company in 2006. His research areas include multi-source feedback, leadership development, high potential engagement, executive on-boarding, and global leadership effectiveness. He works closely with the product development team, providing support for the development of talent management tools and solutions that are research based and experience tested. He earned a Ph.D. in Industrial/Organizational Psychology from Central Michigan University.

Malcolm R. Davies is principal of Learning At Work and was previously founding CEO of the successful brewery start-up, Power Brewing Company Ltd. For 20 years he has specialized in organizational effectiveness, focusing on executive strategy and leadership. In that work Mal has developed innovative approaches to practical organizational challenges. He provides contract CEO, strategy, senior leadership development, executive, and board coaching services, all designed to optimize talent and foster organizational success. Mal holds a Ph.D. in Organizational Psychology from Griffith University and is a registered psychologist. He is based in Brisbane, Australia.

Robert W. Eichinger is Vice Chairman of Korn/Ferry International. He was cofounder and CEO of Lominger Limited and is co-creator of the LEADERSHIP ARCHITECT® Suite of management, executive, and organizational development tools. During his 45+ year career, he has worked inside PepsiCo and Pillsbury, and as a consultant in Fortune 500 companies in many countries. Bob has served on the Board of the Human Resource Planning Society. He holds a Ph.D. in Industrial/Organizational psychology from the University of Minnesota.

William A. Gentry, Ph.D., is currently a Senior Research Associate at the Center for Creative Leadership and also an adjunct assistant professor in the Leadership Studies doctoral program at North Carolina A&T State University. His research interests are in multisource (360-degree) feedback, survey development and analysis, leadership and leadership development across cultures, managerial derailment, and organizational politics and political skill. Bill graduated summa cum laude from Emory University and received his Ph.D. in Applied Psychology from the University of Georgia.

Robert Hogan, Ph.D., president of Hogan Assessment Systems, is an international authority on personality assessment, leadership, and organizational effectiveness. He was McFarlin Professor and Chair of the Department of Psychology at the University of Tulsa for 14 years. Prior to that, he was Professor of Psychology and Social Relations at The Johns Hopkins University. He has received a number of research and teaching awards, is the author of *Personality and the Fate of Organizations* and the Hogan Personality Inventory, and the editor of the *Handbook of Personality Psychology* (Academic Press, 1997). Dr. Hogan received his Ph.D. from the University of California, Berkeley, specializing in personality assessment.

Dr. Hogan is the author of more than 300 journal articles, chapters, and books. He is widely credited with demonstrating how careful attention to personality factors can influence organizational effectiveness in a variety of areas—ranging from organizational climate and leadership, to selection and effective team performance. Dr. Hogan is a fellow of the American Psychological Association and the Society for Industrial/Organizational Psychology.

Robert B. Kaiser is a partner with Kaplan DeVries Inc. and was previously at the Center for Creative Leadership. He has over 100 publications and presentations on leadership, development, and performance measurement. Rob also has a consulting practice; in his coaching work, he grooms high potentials for the executive suite, and in his talent management work he provides research-based services which include developing custom leadership models and assessment tools for organizations and statistical analysis of performance data to inform talent management strategy. He has an M.S. in Industrial/Organizational Psychology from Illinois State University and is based in Greensboro, NC.

Robert E. Kaplan is the founding partner of Kaplan DeVries Inc., a consulting firm specializing in executive development for individuals and teams. He has been working with executives and conducting pioneering research on leadership development since the early 1980s at the Center for Creative Leadership. Bob is the author of many articles and three books; his most recent one, with Rob Kaiser, is *The Versatile Leader: Make the Most of Your Strengths—Without Overdoing It* (Wiley/Pfeiffer, 2006). He has a B.A. and Ph.D. from Yale and is based in New York City.

Jean Brittain Leslie is a Senior Manager in the Tools & Instrument Development Group and a Senior Fellow at The Center for Creative Leadership (CCL) in Greensboro, NC. In this role, she is responsible for architecting, designing, and integrating instruments and tools into CCL and other organizations' leadership development systems. Jean has published over 58 writings on leadership, assessment, and feedback in the form of books, book chapters, peer reviewed articles, and articles in the popular press. She has an M.A. in sociology from the University of North Carolina at Greensboro.

Morgan McCall, winner of the Society for Industrial and Organizational Psychology's 2008 "Distinguished Professional Contributions Award," is a Professor of Management and Organization in the Marshall School of Business at the University of Southern California. His research on the development and derailment of executives has appeared in numerous articles and books, including the trilogy *Developing Global Executives* (Harvard Business Press. 2002), *High Flyers* (Harvard Business Press, 1998), and *The Lessons of Experience* (Lexington Books, 1988). Prior to moving to USC, he held various positions at the Center for Creative Leadership, including Director of Research and Senior Behavioral Scientist.

King Yii Tang is an assistant researcher at Lominger International–A Korn/Ferry Company. Her interests lie in leadership development, teams, personnel selection, 360-degree feedback, and culture. She works closely with the research team on all aspects of research projects and project development. She has a master's degree in Industrial/Organizational Psychology from St. Cloud State University.

Randall P. White is a principal of Executive Development Group, Greensboro, NC, and adjunct faculty with Duke Corporate Education, London. He is the co-author of *Breaking the Glass Ceiling* (Addison-Wesley, 1987) and *Relax, it's Only Uncertainty* (Prentice Hall, 2001). White is a Fellow of the American Psychological Association and a past president of APA's Division 13, Society of Consulting Psychologists. He earned his Ph.D. in developmental sociology from Cornell University.

INTRODUCTION

CHAPTER 1

THE REST OF WHAT YOU NEED TO KNOW ABOUT STRENGTHS-BASED DEVELOPMENT

Robert B. Kaiser
Kaplan DeVries Inc.

In less than a decade positive psychology has grown from an inspired idea on the bank of mainstream psychology to a conceptual sea change in how we think about human development. In many ways this is a welcomed addition. Positive psychology helps round out and balance our approach to individual learning and development. A fair assessment of the first 100 years of the field of psychology is that the emphasis has been on anxiety, illness, and pathology. But critics have pointed out that the good life is about more than the absence of pathology—the things that make life worth living concern growth and fulfillment.

There is much to like about a positive psychology. The founders of the field, Martin Seligman and his colleagues, have presented compelling experimental evidence showing that simple adjustments in your daily life can increase your quality of life in terms of better moods and improved general well-being.[9] Barbara Frederickson[4] has some interesting ideas based on evolutionary theory that explain the good that feeling good can do. Her "broaden-and-build" theory describes how positive emotions widen our perspective and open us up to new knowledge, relationships, and experiences that build intellectual and social capital. As these assets accumulate, we become better able to deal with stiff challenges and complex problems. And more than just an American idea, positive psychology is catching on in Europe through the efforts of thought leaders like Alex Linley and his colleagues at the Centre for Applied Positive Psychology who study people at their best to harvest insights about optimal human functioning.[5]

Strengths-based Development

The contributions of positive psychology, however, stand alongside legitimate questions about how it is being applied in the workplace. Of particular concern is an application known as *strengths-based development.* It was introduced around the turn of the century by Marcus Buckingham and Donald O. Clifton[2] in their book, *Now, Discover Your Strengths*, and has caught on like wildfire. There are a few companies with a significant commercial interest in strengths-based development and they have large marketing machines promoting it to the business world. Their advertising campaigns are effective and have a long reach, as indicated by the flood of strengths-based books in bookstores and on the management best-seller lists.

The central message of the more vocal companies selling the strengths approach is that traditional methods of management training and development are wrong. They claim that a focus on fixing weaknesses is a mistake and a misallocation of time and energy. According to advocates of the strengths movement, to help people become the best they can be, we need to focus on the positives by identifying their natural inclinations and nurturing those talents. A favorite piece of rhetoric is that fixing weaknesses might get you from a "D" to a "C" but will never get you an "A" because the only way to get an "A" is to maximize your innate gifts.

Consider how this message has infiltrated the business press and popular press and influenced conventional wisdom, as exemplified by the following quotes:

"Excellence comes from maximizing strengths, never by fixing weakness."
— USA Today[3]

"[W]hen training is... remedial, it's a waste of time."
— FORTUNE magazine[1]

A Realistic Counterweight

On one hand, it is impressive how effective the champions of the strengths-based approach have been in influencing respected sources like FORTUNE, USA Today, and others. In less than a decade, they have created something approaching a mass movement. And like most mass movements, there is an air of fanatic extremism. Many managers and development professionals have drunk the Kool-Aid, and fervently believe that strengths are all you need.

On the other hand, it is easy to understand the appeal of the message. Who wouldn't prefer to focus on one's upside rather than confront one's downside? There's a bit of a seductive feel-good story in all this. It lets managers off the hook for their shortcomings and says, "It's okay. Don't worry about those problems." Instead managers are encouraged to focus on what they are best at and like to do—what comes naturally and that they enjoy.

And therein lies the problem: when practiced with a single-minded focus, the strengths approach can become an exercise in self-indulgence. It emphasizes what comes easy for managers and what they enjoy doing. What is ignored is what the organization needs from the position that the person's job is designed to provide. It is a case of putting the needs of the individual above the needs of the organization because the job requirements of leadership are not elective, and if managers ignore some, organizational performance will suffer.

In this light, it is no surprise that the strengths-based approach gained its popularity amid the self-serving decadence and delusional optimism of the first decade of the 21st century that spun the global economy out of control. The ensuing crisis was a painful reminder of what happens when self-interest is allowed to reign supreme while wishful thinking obscures hard-nosed reality. At some point, a price must be paid for living the lie that excessive compensation is justified, that hyper-leveraged assets are smart, that toxic securities are risk-free, and that we can afford a mortgage that is well beyond our means. In the same way, a Pollyanna-like devotion to accentuating the positive will eventually reveal itself as a costly mistake.

The point of this book is simple: replacing a one-sided perspective—an obsession with what is wrong—with another one-sided perspective—an exclusive focus on what is right—is misguided and simplistic. Beyond the swinging pendulum of fads and fashion, a better approach to individual growth recognizes that *both* strengths *and* weaknesses have an appropriate place in learning and development.

There is also great folly in the "more is better" mentality behind exhortations to maximize your strengths. Nearly 25 years ago, the seminal *Lessons of Experience*[6] and derailment research by McCall and Lombardo[7] at the Center for Creative Leadership introduced the phrase "strengths become weaknesses" to the managerial vocabulary. It would be unfortunate if these insights became a lost language. But that is what seems to be happening in practice. While some positive psychology scholars are recognizing that strengths—even virtues like courage, compassion, and curiosity—can be overplayed,[8] purveyors of strengths-based development seem to be tone deaf on the point.

Who this Book is for

This book is intended as a cautionary note to supplement popular ideas about strengths-based development. The chapters were written expressly for anyone serious about leadership development. The authors were asked to speak to human resource managers, training professionals, consultants, and executive coaches. The authors also speak directly to managers themselves, in terms of their own development as well as that of their employees. Each chapter presents a distinct point of view in a brief, pithy format with a clear line of sight to action. The chapters are packed with powerful ideas, practical advice, accessible tools, and vivid examples backed by scientific research and extensive experience. What follows is the rest of what you need to know about strengths-based development.

Structure and Content

This volume is organized around three primary sections that are book-ended by an introductory chapter (this chapter) and a capstone summary chapter (chapter 10). The first section takes a careful look at the viability of a purely strengths-based approach to building leaders. The second section focuses on strengths and how strengths can become weaknesses, an ironic truism that is often overlooked in strengths-based development. The final section considers weaknesses and how ignoring them is a lethal strategy for individuals managing their careers, as well as for the organizations building and managing their talent.

Section 1: Strengths-only Is Not Viable

This first section takes two distinctly different data-based approaches to examining the advice that a focus on strengths is sufficient for building the bench strength needed to lead a company to success. First is a chapter by Bob Eichinger, Guangrong Dai, and KingYii Tang of Lominger International. These authors consider how to define a strength, and they distinguish among what one does best, what one does better than other people, and what one does better than others *and* is also aligned with what organizations need from their managers. Then they analyze competency ratings for over 2,000 managers and executives and find that very few managers have five or more competencies at which they are stronger than most other managers. Even fewer have five or more strengths aligned with what organizations need from their mangers to be competitive. The authors conclude that an exclusive reliance on strengths is a weak career strategy. They also conclude that the best bet for driving organizational effectiveness through leadership development is to help leaders become ongoing learners who can regularly sharpen their current strengths and continually acquire new capabilities to meet dynamic business demands and challenges in the global economy.

In the next chapter, Jean Leslie and Anand Chandrasekar of the Center for Creative Leadership report the results of a survey study that compares the skills and competencies that organizations need to be successful to the level of skill that their managers currently possess in those areas. Across three different cultures—the United States, Singapore, and India—they find remarkable similarity in the competencies organizations need most and in the competencies at which managers are most skilled. More importantly, there are major gaps between what organizations need and the strengths their managers bring to the table, and these gaps are quite similar in the U.S., Singapore, and India. These researchers conclude that encouraging managers to maximize their current strengths, to the neglect of developing areas of relative weakness, will inevitably work to the detriment of organizational performance.

The convergent findings from these two studies reveal a major problem with the strengths-based philosophy: in focusing on what individuals are naturally good at, it fails to consider what organizations need from their managers.

Section 2: Strengths Can Become Weaknesses

The second section begins with a chapter from Morgan McCall Jr., author of the celebrated books, *The Lessons of Experience* and *High Flyers*. McCall explains how strengths and weaknesses are not so easy to disentangle. Then, drawing on his research on derailment, developmental experiences, transitions, and expertise, he explains his well-known claim that "strengths can become weaknesses." He illustrates the point by drawing important lessons from examples of high-profile CEO derailments like Phil Condit at Boeing, Carly Fiorina at Hewlett-Packard, and Bob Nardelli at Home Depot. McCall concludes with proven prescriptions for how managers can take a career-long approach to becoming master leaders, including the tips and tricks he has used for years to build leadership bench strength for such firms as Sun Microsystems and IBM.

In the fifth chapter, Rob Kaiser and Bob Kaplan draw on a wealth of experience consulting to senior leaders and data for over 400 upper-level managers based on their innovative 360 tool, the *Leadership Versatility Index®*, to explain how a towering strength can be a mixed blessing. First, they make the point that most managers don't know their strengths. Second, not knowing their strengths, managers are likely to overuse and over-rely on them. Third, in addition to corrupting their strengths, overuse also leads managers to avoid complementary approaches, resulting in a lopsided leadership style. The twin problems of overusing a strength and avoiding complementary approaches are associated with diminished leadership effectiveness and lower performance from the team for which a leader is responsible. Finally, Kaiser and Kaplan provide easy-to-apply concepts, models, and methods you can use to assess and coach leaders to make the most of their strengths—without overdoing it.

The second section concludes with the sixth chapter, by Steven Berglas, a well-known management psychologist. Drawing on his years of research and counseling to senior leaders, Berglas reminds us that most people who make it to the top have an impressive track record resting on a trove of accolades and accomplishments. He further describes how, ironically, a career's worth of success can actually work against these managers when they reach the top, where much is at stake and their leadership matters most. With several anecdotes and an in-depth case analysis of Ken Olsen—the founder of Digital Equipment Corporation who was named American's most successful entrepreneur by FORTUNE magazine six years prior to his forced exit by the Board—Berglas illuminates the dynamics of the dark side of accomplishment and provides solid recommendations for preventing leaders from falling victim to their own success.

Section 3: Weaknesses Matter

The third section takes issue with the naïve notion that weaknesses can be ignored. This section begins with a review by Bill Gentry and Craig Chappelow of lessons learned from over two decades of research at the Center for Creative Leadership on executive derailment. First, they note that experts agree that about half of all senior leaders ultimately derail. They then note the most common causes of derailment, which can often be traced back to a weakness of one kind or another. Their chapter is a brief but invaluable summary of a long program of research and includes suggestions for how to help managers identify risks for derailment and how to turn things around—before it is too late.

The eighth chapter is by Robert Hogan, the leading authority on personality in the workplace who introduced the concept of the "dark side" of personality, and Michael Benson, a former U.S. Air Force major and currently a manager of Leadership Assessment and Development at Johnson & Johnson. Hogan and Benson put positive psychology in the context of personality theory, which they argue is at the heart of understanding leadership. They note that there are two big problems in life: learning to live with oneself and learning to live with others. They then show how positive psychology and offshoots like strengths-based development are primarily concerned with living with oneself. However, leadership is a public act, and foibles, flaws, and idiosyncrasies can be terribly disruptive in relationships with other people. Hogan and Benson offer a catalogue of 11 personality-based reasons for ineffective leadership. They conclude that while it may be an easy sell to tell managers not to worry about their weaknesses, it does those managers a disservice in that weaknesses are the primary determinant of derailment and career failure. The answer they offer is strategic self-awareness—an understanding of how other people experience you, including what they find troubling.

This section concludes with a chapter from Malcolm Davies, an accomplished former CEO-turned-consultant from Australia. Davies puts weaknesses in context and explains how to unlock the value of strengths that are bound up with the dark side personalities that Hogan and Benson discuss. He argues that so-called "toxic" leaders are a small subset of the large percentage of leaders who share "exceptional personality characteristics" that can alternatively be framed as situational strengths. Davies shows how recasting dark side characteristics as situational strengths can facilitate the development of gifted-but-troubling managers by minimizing the inevitable risks associated with these extraordinarily talented individuals. He also describes a model he has used for years to help gifted, but flawed, managers convert the dross of their dark sides into valuable gold.

Conclusion

In the capstone chapter, Randy White—a long-time student and teacher of leadership and former president of Division 13 of the American Psychological Association (the Society for Consulting Psychologists)—takes stock of the preceding chapters to put strengths-based development in perspective. White's chapter is at once insightful, integrative, and witty.

Rather than simply regurgitating what his colleagues have said, he weaves their various strands of thought together with the shuttle of his years of scholarship and the loom of his years of applied experience helping senior executives and corporations around the world develop leadership capacity. The result is White's own unique point of view that pulls into sharp relief the seductive appeal and major weaknesses of a strictly strengths-based approach. The major contribution of his wide-angle perspective is explaining how a focus on strengths promotes stasis and stagnation and inhibits what a wealth of research and experience indicates is the best bet for success: continuous learning and ongoing development.

Final Comment

Let us be clear: the point of this book is not to dismiss strengths-based development. True, we wish to temper the hype that has grown up around it and call attention to the hidden dangers glossed over by some proponents. In doing this, we hope to promote a more balanced approach to developing leaders, an approach that will be more practical and, not insignificantly, much more likely to enhance organizational performance. Our highest hope is that you walk away from this volume as a better-informed consumer of developmental ideas and a savvier user of the strengths-based approach.

References

1. Borden, M., & Buckingham, M. (2000, December 18). Trying to overcome weakness? This man says, 'Please, stop.' *FORTUNE*. Retrieved September 17, 2008, from http://money.cnn.com/magazines/fortune/fortune_archive/2000/12/18/293130/index.htm.

2. Buckingham, M., & Clifton, D. O. (2001). *Now, discover your strengths*. New York: Free Press.

3. Cullen, D. (2001, February 12). Focus on strengths to maximize workers' output. [Review of the book *Now, discover your strengths*]. *USA Today*. Retrieved September 17, 2008, from http://www.usatoday.com/moneybooks/2001-02-12-strengths.htm.

4. Fredrickson, B. L. (2001). The role of positive emotions in positive psychology: The broaden-and-build theory of positive emotions. *American Psychologist*, *56*, 218-226.

5. Linley, A. (2008). *Average to A+: Realising strengths in yourself and others*. Coventry, England: CAPP Press.

6. McCall, W. M., Jr., Lombardo, M., & Morrison, A. (1988). *The lessons of experience*. Lexington, MA: Lexington Books.

7. McCall, W. M., Jr., & Lombardo, M. M. (1983). *Off the track: Why and how successful executives get derailed*. Greensboro, NC: Center for Creative Leadership.

8. Peterson, C. (2006). The Values in Action (VIA) classification of strengths. In M. Csikszentmihalyi & I. S. Csikszentmihalyi (Eds.), *A life worth living: Contributions to positive psychology* (pp. 29-48). New York: Oxford University Press.

9. Seligman, M. E. P., Steen, T., Park, N., & Peterson, C. (2005). Positive psychology progress: Empirical validation of interventions. *American Psychologist, 60*, 410-421.

SECTION 1

Strengths-only is Not Viable

CHAPTER 2

It Depends Upon What You Mean by a Strength

Robert W. Eichinger, Vice Chairman of *Korn/Ferry International*
Guangrong Dai, Lominger International, *A Korn/Ferry Company*
KingYii Tang, Lominger International, *A Korn/Ferry Company*

We are frequently out on the speaking circuit presenting the case for enhanced talent management. The recurring message is that we are all preparing for the second World War for talent. You know the script. Changing demographics—"oldies" are retiring and the "youngies" are taking over. Business is going global. The world is getting flatter. Things are speeding up. Technology changes daily. Industries are consolidating. Everything is getting more complicated.

So jobs are getting bigger, more complex, and global while the pool of talent is shrinking. As if that were not bad enough, CEOs are stumbling at a greater rate.[7] Freshly minted general managers are failing in their first tough assignments. Well studied is that derailment is mostly fueled by a lack of emotional intelligence and learning agility.[6] CFOs are leaving because of the stifling new regulatory environment.[9] So what to do?

Few reject the need for increased attention to managing talent going forward. We haven't run into anyone who thinks things are going well in leadership development. Everyone reports being short on bench strength. Succession planning isn't filling the pipeline.[2] One frequent question we get is some version of "Is it a good idea to have people focus on their strengths instead of addressing weaknesses?"

An Interesting Question

There are two big buzzes rumbling around the competency space. One is the finding that most successful managers and executives have somewhere between five to seven significant strengths around which they build a great career. [6,10] Specifically, they have five to seven of the most mission-critical skills (which usually number between nine and fifteen) for their jobs, have no significant shortcomings in the rest of the mission-critical skills, and have no glaring derailers. That means, as it always has, that no one is expected to have all of the competencies listed on the executive success profile. Success is not a matter of perfection. To succeed, leaders need five to seven of the nine to fifteen competencies that comprise the short list for a typical executive success profile.

The second big buzz in the competency world is the so-called "strengths movement." This movement advises you to find your strengths. Build on your strengths. Fashion a career around your particular strengths. Find a place and a role that plays to your strengths. Work to build your strengths even stronger. Consequently, there's less need to address your weaknesses. It seems to be "all strengths, all the time."

In the midst of this backdrop, two children of one of the authors, both recent college graduates, are asking for career advice. It's the same question high potentials might be asking: "What's the best strategy for planning my career? Should I use the strengths I have and mold my career around them or is there another strategy?"

We wondered, "Is a strengths-based strategy really the best advice?" And being numbers people, we also wondered, "How many people even have enough strengths on which to build a successful career? Is this approach really viable for most people?"

There are both *quantitative* and *qualitative* aspects to analyzing these questions about strengths-based development. The first quantitative question is "How many strengths are enough to be a success?" No one knows for sure, but five seems to be the best guess and is the number the proponents of strength-based development use. Research also suggests that successful executives build a career around five to seven outstanding competencies. So let's say five strengths, and acknowledge that this may be an arbitrary and debatable number.

The qualitative questions begin with determining what counts as a strength. As we will show, there are several ways to think about this matter.

What is a Strength?

We need to be clear about how we define a strength. Most simply stated, strengths might be those talents, skills, and competencies you personally do best. If you need five strengths to succeed, focus on the five things you do better than anything else that relate to your chosen work.

But is that definition sufficient to give the advice to a beginning high potential to find your five strengths and go with them? Are your five best strengths enough to win? Are the five things you do best strong enough to be successful? If your highest grades in school were math, biology and chemistry, but those grades were C's and all your other grades were D's, would you have what it takes for a successful career in science? If your best track and field event was the 100-yard dash, and your best time was 21.6 seconds, is that enough to build an Olympic career around? If your best musical talent is singing and you keep coming in last on American Idol, are you likely to have a successful musical career?

So we wondered how strong your strengths need to be to win? How athletic do you need to be to medal in the Olympics? What ERA stats do you need to be considered a top pitcher? To what level must you develop golf skills in driving, chipping, putting, sand shots, composure under pressure, etc., to win a PGA tournament? How good would you have to be in five job skills to be successful?

While everyone has five personal best strengths (the five skills you are stronger at than all the others), the important question is whether your five personal best strengths really are strong enough to compete and build a career around.

You can't answer that question unless you compare and contrast your five personal best strengths with others you are competing with doing the same work. Who are you competing with? Perhaps it's enough to be in the top 10% of the competitive population, those doing the same job at the same level, to be the best 1 out of 10 doing the work you do. To be the best 10 out of 100 strategists. Upper 10% of negotiators. Top 10% of motivators. Top 10% of team builders. Top 10% of innovators. Top 10 of 100 change managers. The best 1 in 10 executives.

When you are out to create the best department in your industry, what level of talent do you seek when it comes to hiring people? If you aim to achieve the best supply chain efficiency in your industry, what level of talent do you need to design and manage the supply chain? To support the CEO's growth agenda and consistently beat your competition, what level of talent do you need in your key positions? To be the best in your industry, how good would your C-suite team need to be? Do you look for the best of 10? Among the top 3 of 10? Anyone above average?

There are at least two ways to look at strengths. One is what measurement experts call "ipsative"— this refers to what you are personally best at, independent of how strong you are compared to other people. The second way to look at strengths is to compare your strengths to relevant other people; experts call this a "normative" comparison because it considers how strong you are *relative* to an appropriate norm group (i.e., those doing similar kinds of work). We refer to these two ways of defining a strength as "personal best" and "competitive," respectively.

How Many Managers have Five or More Competitive Strengths?

Before you read on, how many managers and executives out of 100 do you think have five competitive strengths, five skills at which they excel compared to their peers?

With this thought in mind, we wanted to see how many people have five competitive strengths compared to the manager/executive population at large. We analyzed 360 assessments of 1,857 individuals who were rated by coworkers on the 67 competencies and skills in our Leadership Architect® model. [5] The sample is described in the sidebar. We asked a simple statistical question: how many individuals have competitive strengths on 5 or more of the 67 competencies? In other words, we wanted to know how many people had five or more competencies which they were better at than most people in the database. In theory, any individual could have 67 competitive strengths, meaning that he or she scored higher than the other 1,856 managers on all 67. And it is possible for a person to have no competitive strengths compared to others. We assumed, as you may have, that many or even most would have five or more competencies on which they excelled relative to other people in the sample.

Since people might have a different idea or standard about what represents a

The analyses reported here were conducted on a data set compiled from 2005 to 2007. The total sample includes assessments of 1,857 individuals made using the Voices® 360-degree survey. The 360 instrument consisted of 67 items designed to assess 67 competencies. The foundation and research on the development of this instrument are summarized in Lombardo and Eichinger.[4,5] Each of the competencies was rated on a 5-point scale to assess how skillful the manager was.

The 1,857 people who were assessed came from 20 different companies representing such industries as manufacturing, media, education, utility, retail, finance, health care and IT. On average, each person was rated by 7 coworkers (1 superior, 3 peers, and 3 subordinates). The gender composition is 62.1% male and 37.9% female and the average age is around 40. The sample represents a broad range of job levels from entry-level managers to executives (specifically: 33.8% supervisor, 35.8% manager, 21.7% director/executive, and 8.8% senior executive). The average number of years of experience in management is 12.6. Over 77.0% have college degrees.

competitive strength, we looked at the top 2% and top 5%—very stringent interpretations of a competitive strength. We also looked at the top 10% and top 15% as more reasonable standards. Finally, we also looked at the top quarter (25%) and top third (33%)—relatively liberal definitions of what might constitute a competitive strength. For what it is worth, we have been asking various audiences what they think is the best definition of a competitive strength and the answer we get most frequently is the upper 10%, in the top 10 out of 100.

The results of our analysis are displayed in Table 1.

As you can see from the results in Table 1, if you use the top 10% as the cutoff or standard to represent a competitive strength, 38.8% of this sample have five or more strengths, and 26.2% of the sample have none. Zero. Zilch. Nada, at least not when a competitive strength is defined as being in the top 10%.

If you use the more stringent definition of top 5% to define competitive strength, then only 18.4% have five or more, and 46.2% have none. If you use the looser, top-quarter definition of a competitive strength, then 77.3% have five or more competitive strengths and 5.2% have none.

Table 1.
Percentage of People with Five or More Strengths at Different Competitive Cutoff Points

Cut-off point			Number of strengths at or above the cutoff point	
Top	Percentile	SDs above Mean	Five or more	None
2%	98th	2.06	5.8%	69.1%
5%	95th	1.65	18.4%	46.2%
10%	90th	1.29	38.8%	26.2%
15%	85th	1.04	56.8%	14.5%
25%	75th	0.68	77.3%	5.2%
33%	67th	0.44	87.3%	2.6%

These are interesting findings. If you have to make a career out of five strengths, *you better first make sure you have five strengths that stand out relative to your peer group*. Many people don't have enough competitive strengths. Some people have none. If they have high career aspirations, they will be disappointed.

So the first answer to one author's children and to aspiring high potentials is that it probably is a good idea to leverage your strengths—if you have enough compared to your competition.

The Strengths that Differentiate

So far, we have distinguished personal best strengths from competitive strengths and examined how many people have five or more competitive strengths. But this begs such questions as just exactly what competitive strengths are we talking about? How common are these strengths? How important are these strengths to success?

Common and Uncommon Strengths

It is important in giving career advice about strengths to consider the particular strengths in question. Career 101 tells us that it is better to leverage those things that you are uniquely good at rather than those things most people, including you, are good at; otherwise your strengths are merely common commodities.

If you have five competitive strengths, but they are the same strengths most others at your level have, then they will not set you apart. On the other hand, if you have five competitive strengths and they are in areas that few people are strong in, you are more distinctive. We call this third definition of a strength a "distinctively competitive" strength.

About one third of the sample (38.8%) has at least five competitive strengths (in the top 10%). What are these strengths? Are these strengths common or uncommon in the population? Will these strengths really differentiate the people who possess them? Using the top 10% as the cutoff point, we identified the 10 most frequent competitive strengths for those who have at least five strengths (shown in Table 2). We then looked at our normative data to see how well the general management and executive population are rated by others on these competencies.

Table 2.
The Ten Most Frequent Competitive Strengths for Those Who Have at Least Five Competitive Strengths

Rank	Most frequent strengths	Common or uncommon
1	Perspective	In the middle
2	Motivating others	Uncommon
3	Strategic agility	In the middle
4	Personal disclosure	Uncommon
5	Customer focus	Common
6	Learning on the fly	Common
7	Comfort around higher management	Common
8	Managing through systems	Uncommon
9	Command skills	Common
10	Ethics and values	Common

Note: The cutoff point for defining a strength was top 10%.

Competencies in the top third are labeled common, those in the lowest third are labeled uncommon. As can be seen in Table 2, 5 of the 10 strengths are common in the population, indicating that the 38.8% of the sample who have 5 competitive strengths are good at something most others are likely to be good at. Only 3 of the top 10 strengths are uncommon, meaning it is unlikely many competitive peers would be good at this.

Who Has the Strengths that Might Matter?

In addition to *personal* best, competitive, and distinctively competitive strengths, there is a fourth, and ultimately most crucial, type of strength: "distinctively competitive and aligned." This refers to what you do better than your peers *and* is also central to succeeding in your job or career. You have to ask yourself, "Are my five top competitive strengths the right ones?" If a third of the population has five competitive strengths (defined as top 10 percent), are those strengths the ones they need to excel as managers and executives? To have a fulfilling career? In other words, it isn't enough to have five competitive strengths unless those strengths are key to being effective. For example, you may be a world-class free-throw shooter, but that won't help you manage an NBA franchise to the championship title.

Following this line of thinking, we next examined how many people in our database have five or more distinctively competitive and aligned strengths. Based on our studies over the last 15 years, we selected eight competencies that repeatedly have been highly correlated with success for managers and executives.[6] These competencies are Creativity, Dealing with Uncertainty and Ambiguity, Building Effective Teams, Innovation Management, Motivating and Inspiring Others, Planning, Strategic Agility, and Managing Vision.

While it may be a matter of debate whether these are *the only* competencies needed for success, few would argue that these eight are not strong candidates for the essential list of competencies for effective managers and executives.

Looking only at these eight competencies, we again went back to our database of managers and executives and asked how many had five or more competitive strengths using the same multiple cutoff scores. The results are shown in Table 3.

Using the top 10% definition for a competitive strength, 3.3% have five of the critical eight, while 66.6% have none of them. Nearly two out of three people in our sample do not have a single competitive and aligned strength. Even using the least stringent definition of a competitive strength (top third), only 24.3% of the sample have five competitive and aligned strengths while 25.0% have none.

So the modified answer to one author's kids and to the high potentials is, "It's a good idea to bank on your strengths if you have five *and* they are strong relative to your peers *and* they are the right five." However, this career advice is of limited value: it only applies to a small minority of people.

Table 3.
Percent of People with Competitive Strengths on Five or More of the Eight Competencies Aligned With Success at Various Cutoff Points

	Cutoff point		Number of competitive and aligned strengths at or above the cutoff point	
Top	Percentile	SDs above Mean	Five or more	None
2%	98th	2.06	0.4%	90.3%
5%	95th	1.65	1.4%	78.8%
10%	90th	1.29	3.3%	66.6%
15%	85th	1.04	6.9%	53.0%
25%	75th	0.68	16.0%	35.6%
33%	67th	0.44	24.3%	25.0%

Strengths across the Hierarchy

As usual, the results in Table 3 led to another question. The leadership pipeline model tells us that career advancement from the bottom to the top involves several documented transitions.[1] Each transition leads to a change in skill requirements. What works in previous positions will not guarantee success at the next level. So we looked at the most frequent competitive strengths (top 10% as cutoff point) for different organizational levels. Those results are shown in Table 4.

The common finding is that the strengths required for success are different at different organizational levels. Similarly, Table 4 shows how the most common strengths are different across the various hierarchical levels. If you select five strengths to concentrate on early in your career as a supervisor, chances are that those skills will no longer be the essential ones required as you move up the career ladder.

A Broader View of Strengths

A likely debate about these findings will be on the definition of a strength and what human characteristics can be called strengths. Some will argue that strengths are innate talents that people are intrinsically either good or bad at that can't be changed much over time. From that perspective, skills and competencies are the behavioral capabilities that build on natural talent and there is not much you can do to improve your lot.

It doesn't sound logical to label a characteristic a strength because it is innate, while labeling another one skill just because it is changeable. From our perspective, it's an issue of "band-width."[8] Specific skills or competencies are behavioral indicators of the second order factors, clusters that are each composed of many specifics skills or competencies and provide a broader dimension of strengths. The 67 competencies in the Leadership Architect® library

Table 4.
Most Common Competitive Strengths across Levels of Current Incumbents

Levels	Most common strengths
Supervisor	Customer focus
	Written communication
	Humor
	Technical learning
Manager	Motivating others
	Personal disclosure
	Conflict management
	Managing through systems
Executive	Ethics and values
	Strategic agility
	Hiring and staffing
	Comfort around higher management
Senior Executive	Managing vision and purpose
	Perspective
	Strategic agility
	Business acumen

Note: Competencies were defined as strengths if an individual's rating was in the top 10% compared to the rest of the sample (greater than 1.29 standard deviations above the average). The competitive strengths in the table are the most frequent ones for each level of management.

roll up to 21 statistically more basic and general clusters, capturing themes such as caring, organizing, relating, presenting, strategizing, and analyzing. If these 21 statistical clusters are the characteristics that better characterize human talents, how likely will individuals have five strengths on these? We repeated the prior analysis on the 21 clusters. Those results are shown in Table 5.

Compared to Table 1, the frequencies are much smaller at the cluster level. If you use the definition of top 10% as the cutoff to represent a competitive strength, 14.6% have five or more strengths, while over half of the sample has none (51.5%). If you broaden your view of strengths, you narrow the number of people who have five truly competitive strengths.

Table 5.
Frequency of People with Five or More Competitive Strengths at the Cluster Level

Cutoff point			Number of "cluster" strengths at or above the cutoff point	
Top	Percentile	SDs above Mean	Five or more	None
2%	98th	2.06	1.6%	88.5%
5%	95th	1.65	6.3%	71.2%
10%	90th	1.29	14.6%	51.5%
15%	85th	1.04	23.6%	37.2%
25%	75th	0.68	43.6%	19.6%
33%	66th	0.44	57.0%	12.4%

The Take-Home Message

In summary, the current data and analyses tell us that few people have five strengths at the competency or the cluster level. Also, it isn't likely that a constant set of strengths will help people build a progressive career path. So kids and high potentials, what is the take-home? First, there are at least four ways to think about strengths: your personal best—which may not be enough to succeed; competitive strengths—skills stronger than most of your competitors; distinctively competitive strengths—which do distinguish you from everybody else, but may not be the keys to success in your job, role, or career; and competitive and aligned strengths—the best bet for long-term career success.

If you plan to succeed by focusing on your strengths, make sure you do more than just discover and build on your strengths (your personal best). You will also need your strengths to stand out compared to your peers (competitive strengths). If you want to stand out among your peers and have a better chance for promotions, make sure your strengths set you apart from other also competitive peers (distinctively competitive strengths). Finally, you had better hope that your five distinctive and competitive strengths include the ones that make a difference when it comes to long-term career success (competitive and aligned strengths).

Our analysis of this data shows that most managers and executives do not have five strengths that are competitive *and* aligned, much less distinctive. That might have something to do with why as many as half of executives stumble, derail, and fail.[3] If our database of over 1,800 individuals from 20 organizations is representative, almost everyone aspiring to significant career growth better start developing things they're not good at now. The way to succeed is to leverage current strengths that matter plus build new ones that matter now and down the career path.

We regularly tell the up-and-coming youngies to first discover their strengths, then gauge how those strengths compare to those of the people they are, and will be, competing with, and finally, find out which strengths they need to fulfill their career dreams and to start working on the ones that are not up to par.

So, use them if you are fortunate enough to have them; build them if you don't.

References

1. Charan, R., Drotter, S., & Noel, J. (2001). *The leadership pipeline*. San Francisco: Jossey-Bass.

2. Conger, J. A., & Fulmer, R. M. (2003). Developing your leadership pipeline. *Harvard Business Review, 81*(12), 76-84.

3. Gentry, W. A., & Chappellow, C. T. (this volume). Managerial derailment: Weaknesses that can be fixed.

4. Lombardo, M. M., & Eichinger, R. W. (2003). *Leadership architect norms and validityreport.* Minneapolis, MN: Lominger Limited, Inc.

5. Lombardo, M. M., & Eichinger, R. W. (2004). *For your improvement: A development and coaching guide* (4th ed.). Minneapolis, MN: Lominger Limited, Inc.

6. Lombardo M. M., & Eichinger, R. W. (2006). *The leadership machine: Architecture to develop leaders for any future* (3rd ed.). Minneapolis, MN: Lominger Limited, Inc.

7. Lucier, C., Schuyt, R., & Tse, E. (2005). CEO succession 2004: The world's most prominent temp workers. *Strategy + Business, 39*, 1-16.

8. Tett, R. P., Guterman, H. A., Bleier, A., & Murphy, P. J. (2000). Development and content validation of a "hyperdimensional" taxonomy of managerial competence. *Human Performance, 13*(3), 205-251.

9. Williams, K. (2007). CFO turnover keeps escalating. *Strategic Finance, 88*(10), 21-22.

10. Zenger, J. H., & Folkman, J. (2002). *The extraordinary leader: Turning good managers into great leaders*. New York: McGraw-Hill.

CHAPTER 3

MANAGERIAL STRENGTHS AND ORGANIZATIONAL NEEDS
A Crucial Leadership Gap

Jean Brittain Leslie & Anand Chandrasekar
Center for Creative Leadership

This chapter considers the intersection of two "hot" topics in talent management mentioned by Eichinger, Dai, and Tang in the prior chapter: a looming leadership gap and assertions that, to become better leaders, managers should focus on their strengths rather than try to fix weaknesses.[3]

The notion of a leadership gap is easy to grasp. First, in the United States, there are the obvious implications arising from a retiring baby-boomer generation that is followed by a younger generation that numbers fewer people. Second, there is an emerging concern that managers do not possess the level of leadership skill that is needed by their organizations now or in the near future. For instance, a Conference Board survey indicated that confidence in leadership bench strength went down from 1997 to 2001. Roughly 50% of respondents to the earlier survey indicated their organization's leadership strength was either excellent or good; this figure dropped to about 33% in 2001.[2] The American Society for Training and Development[1] recently published a survey-based report in which 45% of respondents indicated a leadership skills gap, placing it as a top concern among talent management professionals. Similarly, another large-scale survey found leadership team capability to be the number one human capital issue.[17]

On the surface, a leadership gap may not seem like a burning issue in the context of other pressing organizational challenges and priorities. However, a wealth of research indicates that there are clear links between leadership, employee motivation and performance, and corporate results.[8] Of course, many variables, including those beyond an organization's control, influence organizational performance. Of the variables a company *can* control, however, is leadership, and good leadership can enhance employee engagement. With engaged employees comes increased employee retention, productivity, customer satisfaction, and profitability.[4,7] The linkages connecting leadership to employee engagement and engagement to corporate performance make a leadership gap an urgent concern.

In this chapter, we explore gaps between current and desired levels of leadership skill to address basic questions about the viability of strengths-based development. How widespread is the gap between the strengths leaders possess and the strengths needed for their organizations to succeed? Is this strictly a U.S.-based problem—or is it also a problem in other countries? Which do our data suggest managers focus on to enhance corporate performance—maximizing strengths or shoring up weaknesses?

Leadership Gaps

To address these questions, we analyzed data gathered as part of a research study of 1,723 managers working in 12 financial services and IT companies across three countries (United States, Singapore, and India).*

For our analysis, we relied on previous research on competency-based approaches to leadership effectiveness. Competencies are defined here as persistent characteristics, skills, or behaviors that are needed for effective performance in a job or role.[12,16] The most generalizable competencies for understanding leadership effectiveness are those that cut across many leadership jobs, roles, and functions. The 20 leadership competencies we examined in this research are from a modified version of Benchmarks® (see Table

*The Center for Creative Leadership (CCL) gratefully acknowledges the Singapore Economic Development Board for their support of this research.

1 for definitions). To expose potential gaps between managerial strengths and organizational needs, we compared the relative *importance* managers attributed to leadership competencies with the *current skill level* managers report to be demonstrating.

What the Data Say

To determine what leadership competencies are critical for success, we first examined how U.S. managers rated the competencies in terms of how important they were for organizational performance. Each leadership competency was rated on a 7-point scale with the following anchors: 1 = *Not at all important*, 4 = *Moderately important*, and 7 = *Critically important*. The column in Table 2 labeled *% Rated as important* presents the percentage of managers who rated a given competency as a 6 or 7 on the 7-point importance

Data reported in this article were collected between January 2006 and December 2007. The sample is largely male (69%) and the average age is 42. The managers' organizational levels include 5% top executive (responsible for entire business; e.g., CEO, CFO, COO, CIO); 12% senior executive (oversee multiple departments/units); 33% upper-middle manager (heads of functions or departments); and 50% middle (have groups reporting to me, but I report to a function head).

Data were collected using a modified version of Benchmarks®, a 360-degree tool that assesses characteristics associated with executive success.[11]

scale. Note that the competencies are ranked from those most frequently rated a 6 or 7 on importance to those least frequently rated that high in terms of importance. This speaks to the leadership competencies most needed for organizations to succeed.

Table 1.
Definitions of competencies used in this research

Competency	Definition
Balancing personal life & work	Balancing work priorities with personal life so that neither is neglected
Building & mending relationships	Responding to coworkers and external parties diplomatically
Managing your career	Using professional relationships (such as networking, coaching, and mentoring) to promote one's career
Managing change	Using effective strategies to facilitate organizational change
Compassion & sensitivity	Showing understanding of human needs
Confronting people	Acting resolutely when dealing with problems
Decisiveness	Preferring doing or acting over thinking about the situation

(Table 1 cont. next page)

Table 1. (cont.)

Respecting individuals' differences	Effectively working with and treating people of varying backgrounds (culture, gender, age, educational background) and perspectives fairly
Doing whatever it takes	Persevering under adverse conditions
Leading people	Directing and motivating people
Participative management	Involving others (such as listening, communicating, informing) in critical initiatives
Putting people at ease	Displaying warmth and using humor appropriately
Being a quick learner	Quickly learning new technical or business knowledge
Resourceful	Working effectively with top management
Self-awareness	Recognizing personal limits and strengths
Composed	Remaining calm during difficult times
Employee development	Coaching and encouraging employees to develop in their careers
Strategic planning	Translating vision into realistic business strategies including long-term objectives
Culturally adaptable	Adjusting to ethnic/regional expectations regarding Human Resource practices and effective team processes
Inspiring commitment	Recognizing and rewarding employees' achievements

We next considered the extent to which leaders can perform these important competencies by analyzing the managers' ratings of their current skill level. Each leadership skill was rated on a 9-point scale with the following anchors: 1 = *Extremely small amount*, 5 = *Moderate amount*, and 9 = *Extremely large amount*. The column of Table 2 labeled *Current Skill Level* presents the average skill rating for each competency.

Comparing the rank-order of the importance of competencies to the amount of skill managers report possessing reveals a major disconnect. Only 5 of the competencies rated in the top 10 most important were also rated in the top 10 in terms of current skill level (*Resourceful, Participative management, Being a quick learner, Doing whatever it takes*, and *Respecting individuals' differences*). In other words, many of the competencies most important for organizational success are not the competencies at which managers are most skilled. The biggest leadership gaps are in the areas of *Strategic planning, Managing change, Employee development* and *Inspiring commitment*, which are very similar to the competencies that Eichinger, Dai, and Tang described in the previous chapter as *distinctively competitive and aligned* (competencies that are highly related to leadership effectiveness but in short supply). More striking, *Leading people*—the competency rated most important for organizational success in the current study—was ranked a poor 13th out of 20 in terms of current skill level.

Table 2.
U.S. managers' ratings of the importance of leadership competencies and their current skill level

Competency	% Rated as Important[1]	Current Skill Level[2]
1. Leading people	88	5.80
2. Strategic planning	84	5.51
3. Managing change	81	5.48
4. Resourceful	79	6.27
5. Inspiring commitment	81	5.64
6. Participative management	81	6.00
7. Being a quick learner	76	6.40
8. Doing whatever it takes	77	6.82
9. Employee development	76	5.35
10. Respecting individuals' differences	72	6.86
11. Balancing personal life and work	73	5.79
12. Building and mending relationships	71	6.15
13. Decisiveness	71	5.99
14. Composed	71	6.42
15. Confronting people	69	5.73
16. Self-awareness	67	5.90
17. Culturally adaptable	65	6.53
18. Managing one's career	65	5.31
19. Compassion and sensitivity	65	6.28
20. Putting people at ease	52	6.03

Notes: [1]Competencies were considered important if they were rated as a 6 or 7 on the 7-point scale in terms of importance to organizational performance. [2]Current skill level was rated on a 9-point scale where 1 = *Extremely small amount* and 9 = *Extremely large amount*

Looking at the question from the perspective of current skill levels, our results show how many leaders have strengths in areas that are not most important for success. *Putting people at ease*, for example, was rated important for success by only 52% of the managers surveyed, yet managers rated it as the 9th most developed skill of the 20 competencies. *Putting people at ease* concerns making others relaxed and comfortable in your presence. CCL research shows this competency is related to the impulse control and positive/optimistic aspects of emotional intelligence.[15] Managers who are skilled in this area can appropriately manage negative emotions like anger that de-motivate and make employees uncomfortable.

Interestingly, the ability to confront problem employees (*Confronting people*) is a relative weakness, rated in the bottom half in terms of skill level, and is also in the bottom half in terms of importance to organizational success. However, taking action with non-performers is one of the more difficult tasks for a manager and failure to deal with problem employees is a common reason for derailment.[5] At best, failure to deal with problem employees undermines the morale and motivation of the rest of the team. At worst, it can increase turnover and damage productivity.

Cross-cultural Consistency

To determine whether these leadership gaps are common across cultures or confined to the U.S., we analyzed comparable survey data collected from 953 managers working in Singapore and 442 managers working in India. Compared to the U.S. data, strikingly similar gaps between importance and skill ratings for the 20 competencies were found in both countries. Comparing the importance that managers in Singapore and India placed on the 20 leadership competencies, we found a considerable overlap with the competencies that U.S. managers' rated as important. Specifically, 8 out of the top 10 leadership competencies identified as most important in the U.S. are also in the top 10 most important for Singapore and India.

Table 3.
Top 10 competencies rated as important to organizational success in Singapore and India

Singapore	India
1. Leading people	1. Strategic planning
2. Inspiring commitment	2. Leading people
3. Managing change	3. Inspiring commitment
4. Strategic planning	4. Being a quick learner
5. Resourceful	5. Resourceful
6. Participative management	6. Managing change
7. Employee development	7. Employee development
8. Balancing personal life and work	8. Participative management
9. Being a quick learner	9. Doing whatever it takes
10. Building and mending relationships	10. Decisiveness

The next question we considered was the amount of skill managers in Singapore and India report compared to managers in the U.S. We found that 7 of the top 10 most skilled competencies in the American sample were also in the top 10 most skilled competencies in the samples from Singapore and India. With ratings of importance and strengths fairly similar across the three countries, it is evident that a clear and perhaps universal gap exists in terms of leadership capacity.

The extent to which we found similar and pervasive leadership gaps across three distinctly different cultures may strike some as surprising. The Global Leadership and Organizational Behavior Effectiveness (GLOBE) research project found cultural values and leadership styles in Singapore to be influenced by both the East and the West.[10]

Table 4.

Top 10 competencies in terms of current skill level among managers in Singapore and India

Singapore	India
1. Doing whatever it takes	1. Resourceful
2. Respecting individuals' differences	2. Composed
3. Resourceful	3. Doing whatever it takes
4. Being a quick learner	4. Culturally adaptable
5. Culturally adaptable	5. Self-awareness
6. Compassion and sensitivity	6. Compassion and sensitivity
7. Composed	7. Respecting individuals' differences
8. Building and mending relationships	8. Being a quick learner
9. Participative management	9. Inspiring commitment
10. Self-awareness	10. Leading people

More specifically, Singapore scored higher than other Confucian Asian countries on participative leadership, team orientation, and humane leadership. Perhaps these perceptions account for some of the similarities found in the relative importance of select competencies. In addition to examining leadership in Singapore, GLOBE researchers reported the attributes of outstanding managers in India.[6] Many of the characteristics are similar to those we would find among outstanding managers in the U.S. An outstanding manager in India is, for example, inspiring, visionary, a good communicator, decisive, and resourceful— many of the competencies rated as important in the U.S. Given this agreement in the relative importance of various leadership competencies, the perceived need for skill development in these critical areas is cause for alarm.

Future Leadership Skill Needs

Our survey asked respondents to rate each of the 20 leadership competencies according to the current level of skill managers in their organizations are demonstrating as well as what level of skill was needed to be maximally effective. We compared ratings of *needed skill* levels to ratings of *current skill* levels and found that managers in the U.S., Singapore, and India believe they need to be more skilled on all 20 competencies, not less. Had we not asked the question about needed skill levels we would have missed an important finding. Even though there is a range in managers' current leadership skills where certain areas are strengths, they expect to need much more skill in the future. These data make the case for focusing on both strengths and development needs—that is, current well-developed skills need to be enhanced while areas of relative weakness also need to be shored up.

Implications

There are two major implications from this survey study. First, an exclusive focus on strengths in leadership development is insufficient. Second, closing the leadership gap requires that we do a better job of aligning the focus of development with organizational needs.

A Strengths-only Approach Isn't Viable

The view that managers can best benefit their organizations by focusing on their strengths is not supported by our data. The skills most prevalent among managers—that is, their current strengths—are not the same as the skills that are most critical to organizational performance. If we're going to tell managers to rely on their strengths, there's good cause for concern that they would be applying the wrong skills. This is consistent with the results of a prior analysis of CCL's assessment database.[9] The data in that study, collected between June 2000 and November 2004, included 360-degree feedback ratings for nearly 40,000 managers from 361,901 coworkers and 36,399 direct bosses. More than 7,500 organizations, including many *Fortune 500* companies, were represented. The results were shocking. A comparison of what managers' bosses perceived as critical to organizational success and what coworkers judged managers to be skilled at revealed massive gaps like those in the present study. In other words, what managers believe to be important for their organizations' success is typically not rated by coworkers as a strength that managers in fact posses. For example, coworkers' evaluations of the ability of managers in terms of leading people—the competency deemed most important to organizational success in both the previous study and the present study—was the second lowest-rated competency in terms of current skill level. As another example, while bosses saw the ability to delegate, motivate, and develop others as being very important, on balance managers were judged to be relatively weak in this skill.

Both of these studies show how focusing solely on one's strengths may not meet the needs of the organization. Of course, it is important for people to appreciate their strengths and understand how to leverage them. But this individual-oriented view also needs to be counter-balanced by consideration for what the organization needs from its cadre of managers and leaders. This pulls into sharp relief the Achilles' heel of the current strengths movement: in focusing on the skills that are rewarding, natural, and easiest for individuals to master, this movement overlooks what organizations require for success.

Closing the Leadership Gap

Closing the leadership gap means aligning the development needs of managers with organizational objectives. Despite the billions of dollars pumped into leadership development each year, many organizations are unable to close their leadership gaps. While there is a demonstrated link between a company's ability to provide leaders with the development opportunities they most value and the overall strength of the leadership pipeline,[13] many organizations lack a coherent sense of what needs to be developed and how to go about it. CCL has elaborated a model for doing this. Below are five processes organizations can put into place to help with successful talent management. For more on these processes and larger models for linking leadership development to organizational development, see *The Leadership Gap: Building Leadership Capacity for Competitive Advantage*[18] and *The Strategic Development of Talent.*[14]

- Perform a needs assessment. Identify the capabilities managers need now *and in the future* to execute and sustain the organization's strategy.

- Develop clear, specific goals and strategies for individual leadership development. Assess managers' strengths and weaknesses against the core competencies identified in the needs assessment.

- Excel at recruiting, identifying, and developing talent, performance management and retention.

- Evaluate how well these efforts are paying off across the organization. What additional resources are needed? What metrics are in place to assess impact?

- Provide a continuous loop of feedback, coaching, and assessment towards goal attainment.

References

1. American Society for Training and Development (ASTD) Public Policy Counsel (2006, Fall). *Bridging the skills gap: How the skills shortage threatens growth and competitiveness...and what to do about it*. Alexandria, VA: ASTD Publications Department.

2. Barrett, A., & Beeson, J. (2002). *Developing business leaders for 2010*. New York: The Conference Board.

3. Buckingham, M., & Clifton, D. O. (2001). *Now, discover your strengths*. New York: Free Press.

4. Buckingham, M., & Coffman, C. (1999). *First, break all the rules*. New York: Simon & Schuster.

5. Charan, R., & Colvin, G. (1999, June 21). Why CEO's fail. *Fortune*, 69-82.

6. Chhokar , J. S. (2007). India: diversity and complexity in action. In J. S. Chhokar, F. C. Brodbeck, & R. J. House (Eds.), *Culture and leadership across the world* (pp.971-1020). Mahwah, New Jersey: Lawrence Erlbaum Associates, Publishers.

7. Harter, J. K., Schmidt, F. L., & Hayes, T. L. (2002). Business-unit-level relationship between employee satisfaction, employee engagement, and business outcomes: A meta-analysis. *Journal of Applied Psychology, 87*, 268-279.

8. Kaiser, R. B., Hogan, R., & Craig, S. B. (2008). Leadership and the fate of organizations. *American Psychologist, 63*, 96-110.

9. Leslie, J. B., & Taylor, S. (2005, January/February). The negatives of focusing only on the positive. *Leadership in Action,24*(6), 19-20.

10. Li, J., Ngin, P. M., & Teo, A. C. (2007). Culture and leadership in Singapore: combination of the East and the West. In J. S. Chhokar, F. C. Brodbeck, & R. J. House (Eds.), *Culture and leadership across the world* (pp. 947-963). Mahwal, New Jersey: Lawrence Erlbaum Associates, Publishers.

11. Lombardo, M. M., McCauley, C. D., McDonald-Mann, D., & Leslie, J. B. (1999). *Benchmarks® developmental reference points*. Greensboro, NC: Center for Creative Leadership.

12. Meger, B. (1996) A critical review of competency-based systems. *The Human Resource Professional, 9*(1), 22-25.

13. Michaels, E., Handfield-Jones, H., & Axelrod, B. (2001). *The war for talent*. Boston: Harvard Business School Press.

14. Rothwell, W. J. & Kazanas H. C. (2003). *The strategic development of talent*. Massachusetts: HRD Press, Inc.

15. Ruderman, M. N., Hannum, K., Leslie, J. B., & Steed, J. L. (2003). Emotional intelligence and career derailment. *Competency & Emotional Intelligence, 10*(3), 39-41.

16. Spencer, L. M. & Spencer, S. M. (1993). *Competence at work: Models for superior performance*. New York: John Wiley & Sons.

17.   Weiss, D., & Finn, R. (2005). HR metrics that count. *Human Resources Planning, 28*(1), 33-38.

18.   Weiss, D., & Molinaro, D. (2005). *The leadership gap: Bridging leadership capability for competitive advantage.* Mississauga, ON, Canada: John Wiley & Sons.

SECTION 2

Strengths Can Become Weaknesses

CHAPTER 4

EVERY STRENGTH A WEAKNESS AND OTHER CAVEATS

Morgan W. McCall, Jr.
Marshall School of Business
University of Southern California

Make things as simple as possible, but not simpler.
— Albert Einstein

Everyone who has ever tried to change someone else's behavior—or for that matter, their own—knows it can be a difficult proposition. Perhaps this is because of a general human tendency toward an enhancement bias in self-perception. The evolutionary psychologist, Steven Pinker, observed that "people consistently overrate their own skill, honesty, generosity, and autonomy" as well as "overestimate their contribution to a joint effort, [and] chalk up their successes to skill and their failures to luck."[30] With these forces in play, the odds of people accepting negative feedback and agreeing to change appear long indeed. Add to that the findings of a recent survey that "90% of managers think they're among the top 10% of performers in their workplace,"[7] and it is not surprising that bosses might be quick to embrace any alternative to confronting their subordinates' weaknesses.

As if an answer to the unspoken prayer, the recent emphasis on "playing people to their strengths" provides just such an escape. It is difficult to fix people, the theory goes, so it is better to focus on making more effective use of their proven strengths. It sounds simple, and may be an effective strategy for some outstanding football quarterbacks, world-class quarter milers, and champion chess masters (actually it isn't, but more on that later). But this approach may not work as well for those in, or aspiring to, leadership roles. For them that strategy is overly simple and, as we will see, even may jeopardize their careers.

The idea that people should be played to their strengths has deep roots. Long ago in some cultures it was believed that everyone was put on this earth for a specific reason. It was thought that each of us had a special gift, called a "genius," and our purpose in life was to bring that gift into the world (a process sometimes aided by an obsessive "mentor" who recognized the gift and was therefore obligated to see to it that it was brought forth). Obviously there was a single-minded focus on the strength inherent in the genius, and often a whole village was committed to seeing it through.

Fast forward to more modern times when leadership was viewed in a similar way—the "genius" possessed by "great men" who shaped great events. (The word "genius" derived from the Latin word meaning guardian spirit or, later, natural talent. It's not far from there to seeing talent as "genetic.") This notion feeds the belief that leaders are born that way, that they have unique strengths (once called "towering strengths" at PepsiCo) that, if not outright gifts, are natural talents that were nurtured early on. From this perspective, as with genius in earlier times, it is rational to emphasize those strengths.

The unstated but logical corollary is that skills that do not derive from innate gifts cannot become "towering strengths," and outright weaknesses can not be turned into strengths through learning, experience, and development. The best strategy, therefore, is to build on one's strengths rather than to mess much with the other stuff. However, if leadership skills can be developed and if flaws can be corrected or mediated—in other words, if people can learn, grow, and change—then perhaps focusing narrowly on existing strengths is not the best strategy.

Recent progress in neuroscience and in genetics sheds some light on the issue of talent and change. From neuroscience, for example, we know that the brain itself is changed by experience (and sometimes just by observation of other people[16]). If experience is powerful enough to change the structure of the brain, then certainly we aren't totally constrained by the wiring we bring into the world.

Twin studies have looked specifically at the relationship between heredity and the number of leadership-related roles held ("leadership role occupancy"). The results suggest that approximately 30% of the variance in holding leadership roles is attributable to genetic factors.[1,2] Some may interpret the 30% figure as evidence that leadership is largely a gift. While 30% is not trivial, the fact is that a larger chunk of the variance is explained by environmental factors, especially experience. To the extent that leadership strengths are acquired and sharpened on the job, these findings suggest that many strengths are learned from experience and not simply native gifts.

Taken together, the neuroscience and genetic research seem to warrant at least two conclusions. First, in the leadership arena, even with such a crude criterion as "number of leadership positions held," the natural gifts one brings to the party are not enough—70% of what separates leaders from followers is acquired some other way. Second, people can and do change in profound ways, even to the point of rewiring the brain, and therefore can develop new strengths as well as correct weaknesses.

Having established that leaders are not necessarily limited by their natural strengths, we can take a closer look at other assumptions underlying the strengths-based approach to leadership development. Four areas of research are relevant: why talented executives and managers sometimes derail; the transitions required for career success; how executives develop through experience; and the acquisition of expertise. All four research streams support the conclusion that relying on strengths is a dubious strategy in the world of corporate leadership.

Derailment

Two assumptions underlying a strategy of playing people to their strengths are questionable in light of what we know about derailed executives. (A derailment is said to occur when successful managers, expected to continue being successful, are instead fired, demoted, or stalled.) First is the assumption that a strength is a strength is a strength. The second is the assumption that weaknesses can be neglected either because people's strengths are sufficient to offset them, or because people can avoid situations where their dark sides cause them serious trouble. Research on derailment dating as far back as 1983 raises serious questions about these assumptions.[27] If strengths aren't always strengths—if indeed every strength can be a weaknesses—then playing to them can magnify rather than overshadow weaknesses. If situations in which weaknesses are problematic can't be avoided, then those weaknesses, rather than strengths, could become the more important factor in determining success or failure.

There is good reason to believe that both dynamics are not only possible but are relatively common. In trying to understand why talented people sometimes derail, we identified four dynamics that are relevant to the present argument: Strengths become weaknesses, flaws matter, arrogance takes over, and bad luck happens.[25]

Strengths Become Weaknesses

Strengths that have led to success, the very ones that advocates claim should be played to, can become weaknesses over time or in a new situation. Take, for example, the cofounder and former chief executive officer of Sun Microsystems, Scott McNealy. Prior to the bursting of the technobubble, he was widely admired as the underdog maverick willing to take on the dominance of Microsoft and IBM. Who could ever forget the sight of Bill Gates rocking uncomfortably before Congress as McNealy made his statement? Yet, as reported in *BusinessWeek*,[22] "His greatest strengths...turned out to be critical flaws. [His] high-minded resolve began to look to others like simple-minded obstinacy." Here is a case where the very strengths that made him an heroic character eventually prevented him from making the changes that were required to keep the company successful.

Or take the case of former Boeing CEO, Phil Condit. After a brilliant career as an engineer, eventually reaching the top position, he derailed for a variety of reasons that included alleged ethical lapses. But the aspect that interests us most in this context was the observation that "the skills that made him a brilliant engineer—obsessive problem solving and an ability to envision elegant design solutions—were of less use in an executive position."[18] What does it mean that his strengths "were of less use"? Perhaps it suggests that as an executive he needed different skills; that the ones that had made him a successful engineer and were in large part responsible for his promotion to the top job were no longer effective in dealing with the problems of this office. And, perhaps, the more he used those less-than-useful skills (under stress we tend to go back to what has made us successful[14]), the more he was distracted from doing what needed to be done.

In short, both of these CEOs needed *different* strengths to stay successful as their circumstances changed over time. Strengths can be overused, used when they are no longer the ones needed in the situation, or literally become flaws in situations requiring a different skill-set. How might things have been different had they acquired new strengths along the way rather than clinging to, and over-relying on, what had made them successful in the past?

As situations change, the development of new strengths (and often the letting go of old ones) may be required. People are inclined to stick with their strengths (and the more successful they are, the more likely people are to stay with doing what they know), and organizations, rational as they are, like to keep people doing what they are good at. Unfortunately, development requires doing things people don't yet know how to do, so playing people to their strengths only looks like an effective strategy until the situation changes and the old strengths no longer serve.

Flaws Matter

Ignoring, neglecting, or overlooking their people's flaws spares managers the painful and difficult task of trying to fix them. It does not, however, spare flawed people from being derailed by their flaws. There are at least two reasons that it is foolish to ignore flaws, as difficult as they may be to change. First, every one of us has flaws. While it is true that "towering" strengths can overshadow flaws and even lead to forgiving them, the changing situations that can negate strengths can also inflame flaws. It's hard to imagine, for example, that the board was unaware that controversial former CEO Carly Fiorina had a few flaws that could, in the Hewlett-Packard culture, be her undoing. But her "charisma and confidence" that promised to reform Hewlett-Packard seemingly led the decision makers to miss that her existing flaws, notably her rock star craving for the limelight, would become salient in an engineering-oriented culture.[31]

The second reason it is dangerous to ignore flaws is that they frequently camouflage themselves as strengths. An autocrat who gets results may be seen as demanding or having high standards; a person incapable of making a decision might be seen as a consensus builder or excellent listener. Because flaws may also be strengths (it's often a matter of degree), they can be difficult to self-assess and to change, but the danger here is that they may appear to be the very strengths that we are advised to play to. Reinforcing them in turn may make people less aware of the impact of their behavior while at the same time encouraging them to become more extreme.

Success Leads to Arrogance

While we all strive to be successful, success is not without its negative consequences. The confidence required to take on challenges is reinforced by meeting those challenges. All too often, however, confidence ceases to be a strength when it slides into arrogance. Success after success can result in a loss of humility (for more on this dynamic, see chapter 6 by Steven Berglas).[3]

Carly Fiorina's hubris no doubt played a part in alienating her support on the H-P board and within the company, yet its soul mate, confidence, no doubt contributed to her many achievements. While this is an extreme case of a strength (self-confidence) becoming a weakness (arrogance), it is a frequent dynamic among the very successful who derail. Arrogance does its dirty work when people believe their strengths are greater than they are, that their strengths will always carry them, or that they don't need to do anything about their dark side. It's not much of a stretch to see that for successful people, emphasizing their strengths and not confronting their flaws would fertilize the growth of this disease.

Bad Luck

It might appear that when bad luck leads to derailment there is no message about strengths or weaknesses: stuff happens. However, when bad luck occurs, existing strengths may not be enough to remedy things, or untended flaws may flare up, making matters considerably worse. In other words, bad luck creates a new situation in which one's perceived strengths and weaknesses play out differently.

In sum, people are complex tapestries of strengths and weaknesses, and understanding their success or derailment requires considering *combinations* of strengths and weaknesses in specific contexts. Strengths can be overplayed or become irrelevant; strengths in combination with certain flaws may be benign in one situation but lethal in another; arrogance resulting from towering strengths can lead to failure. In short, there is no such thing as an unqualified strength, and any effective development strategy will have to acknowledge that what matters are combinations of strengths and weaknesses as they manifest themselves in specific situations.

Transitions

It is clear from the discussion of the dynamics of derailment that a key trigger for misfortune is change. If everything remained the same, the person and the situation, then whatever set of strengths was effective in that situation would never need to change. It would be a sensible strategy to focus on those strengths and reinforce them. However, it is highly unlikely that both a person and the situation will stay the same over time. Thresholds, transitions, passages, stages, whatever words we choose, are integral to life itself. In traditional societies these transitions were marked by "rites of passage" or "rites of initiation" that included various rituals and ceremonies aimed at producing "a basic change in existential condition: the novice emerges from his ordeal endowed with a totally different being from that which he possessed before his initiation."[10] Rituals punctuated life's passages, those places where people need "to separate and to be reunited, to change form and condition, to die and to be reborn."[33]

The transition to adulthood was one occasion for a rite of passage in which the child went through an intense ritual, sometimes even risking death, to emerge on the other side as a man or woman. An occasion was created to shed those strengths that made the successful child, as well as to transcend those flaws that might prevent the child from becoming a successful adult.

The point is that neither people nor situations remain the same, and even though modern societies have long since discontinued serious rituals to mark many of life's transitions, the requirement to cross thresholds remains. Psychologists refer to them as life stages or passages,[4,13,23] and similar notions emerged in the managerial world in books like *Leadership Passages: The Personal and Professional Transitions that Make or Break a Leader*[9] and *Managerial Lives in Transition: Advancing Age and Changing Times*.[19] In all of these cases, the theme is giving up the old and moving into something new (see Arthur Freedman's Pathways-and-Crossroads model for a practical psychological model of helping managers with such a process).[14] Deny it as we might, to play people to existing strengths in a world requiring transitions would prevent them from moving to the next level.

In the world of work, particularly managerial work, transitions play a major role. David Dotlich and his colleagues, for example, identify 13 passages that senior leaders described to them, which they call passages because "they take you from one place to another; you see the world and yourself differently after you've gone through the events and emotional states that define each passage."[9] Sound familiar? The events they describe, including such things as bad bosses, losing a job, becoming a leader, etc., share a common characteristic: "Learning from a passage, however, isn't possible unless you let go of your past assumptions. In other words, you must admit that some of the very attributes, qualities, attitudes, and skills that made you successful in the past won't necessarily make you successful in the future and that your old knowledge may no longer be applicable."[9] In other words, emphasizing existing strengths, while comfortable, will not get a person successfully through a passage. Not only are new skills and knowledge required, but old ones must be let go of!

Linda Hill's[17] classic study of the transition from individual contributor to manager, for example, found that "becoming a manager" required both a psychological shift and giving up strengths that had served the individual contributors well. "The new managers," Hill says, "described the transformation vividly, weaving tales of coping with the stresses of transformation, reluctantly letting go of deeply held attitudes and habits, and timidly experimenting with new ways of thinking and being."[17] There is no clearer statement of the importance of giving up what has made one successful and, at the same time, acquiring new strengths. To stay with what worked prior to taking a managerial role, even if those qualities were the reasons for the promotion, would almost certainly guarantee failure because the first managerial assignment "involves a transformation—a fundamental change in identity and point of view."[17]

At higher managerial levels, relevant prior experience matters for success in making the transition to general manager. Jack Gabarro,[15] in one of the few empirical studies of its kind, showed that for new general managers "taking charge" in a new role, existing strengths guided their initial actions but were not adequate and even could be detrimental as time went on. In his conclusion he points out that "development results from being stretched and *acquiring added skills*, perspective, and judgment."[15] Clearly, existing strengths are not enough to make this transition successfully, thus the emphasis on adding to them. What is unsaid, yet unassailable, is that those with less than relevant prior experience must let go of what that experience has taught them or fail to recognize how the transition has presented them with different challenges that require a change in perspective and different skills.[32]

McCall and Hollenbeck, in a study of global executives living and working in foreign cultures, found that what was a strength in one culture could become a decided disadvantage in a different one. Giving corporate meaning to the Greek *areté hamartia* (your unique excellence becomes your fatal flaw), they described global derailments in seemingly paradoxical terms:

> This one derailed because of "insufferable arrogance," but that one derailed for being too humble. "Too Swedish," one executive said of a derailed colleague. This one was so mired in detail as to miss the possibilities, while that one was too visionary to get anything done. One was an imperious autocrat; the other delegated too much. One was overly analytical, but the next one was unfocused and not analytical enough. Didn't keep promises; didn't let go of promises that didn't work out. Couldn't achieve consensus, or achieved consensus by surrounding himself with yes-men.[26]

Their conclusion was that context was everything in understanding failures in international work. What worked splendidly in one culture could bring disaster in the next. Global transitions required reassessing, sometimes letting go, sometimes adding to, sometimes both, but rarely staying the course.

When Ram Charan and his associates postulated that there are "six career passages or pipeline turns" in the organizational hierarchy that each involve "a major change in job requirements, demanding new skills, time applications, and work values,"[5] they found the sweet spot in organizational efforts to develop managerial talent. The popularity of their book, *The Leadership Pipeline*, reflects the common experience of corporations that there are successive transitions in a leadership career, beginning with the change from individual contributor to manager (see Linda Hill's work described earlier),[17] and progressing through managing managers, managing functions, managing a business, group manager, and finally enterprise manager. What they argue is that each of these passages "requires that people acquire a new way of managing and leading and leave the old ways behind…"[5] Note the repetitious theme of letting go of the old and acquiring the new. Failure to do so, they suggest, results in a clogged leadership pipeline:

> Imagine a company where more than half the managers at each turn are operating with skills, time applications, and values inappropriate to their level; either they've skipped a level and never learned what they need to know or they're clinging to an old mode of managing that was successful for them in the past. [5]

They go on to say that "jammed pipelines are often filled with managers who can't let go of behaviors that made them successful at lower leadership levels."[5] Successful negotiation of a passage, they point out, requires people to reinvent themselves.

This is true of transitions in general; they typically require an individual to negotiate three stages: separation (letting go of the old), ambiguity (being neither what you were nor what you will be), and integration (becoming something different). That these stages are difficult is why in other times rituals forced people at transition points to let go of the past so that new strengths could emerge.

Development through Experience

As if research on derailment and transitions weren't convincing enough, relying on existing strengths also is contrary to findings about how managers and executives develop through experience.[27,28] Different kinds of experiences (for example, start ups versus turnarounds or domestic versus global jobs) teach different lessons, implying that different strengths are necessary to successfully meet the different kinds of challenges embedded in the experiences. Consistent with both the derailment dynamics and the demands of transitions, different kinds of experiences represent new situations that change how and in what ways strengths and weaknesses play out. Only as long as people stay in situations where what they know how to do is sufficient is there little need to develop different strengths or to worry about flaws.

As an example, serial entrepreneurs go from start-up to start-up and never have to develop the skills to run anything once it is established. The same is true for turnaround specialists who move from one broken business to another (or "break" functioning businesses so they can use their fix-it skills), never needing to develop the skills required to start something new or to grow something that is doing well. These are clear cases of playing to strengths, and the strategy might be successful as long as the start-ups and the turnarounds remain essentially the same. But as soon as a person is called upon to deal with a fundamentally different situation, and as leadership roles become more complex, the ability to draw on *many* different strengths becomes increasingly important. To make matters worse, using some of the skills effective in one type of leadership challenge (e.g. a start-up) may prove disastrous in another type (e.g. a turnaround). So once again we end up seeing the importance of adding new strengths and letting go of some of the old ones, rather than sticking with what one already knows.

But the research on experience-as-teacher takes us one step further. Powerful experiences teach negative as well as positive lessons. People who undertake repeated turnarounds, for example, tend to lose their compassion because closing facilities and laying off people are psychologically painful. Getting through it, repeatedly, can require a person to find psychological distance. Repeated start-ups, like heroin, are addictive: people who enjoy the high can grow intolerant and bored of the routine of a well-run organization. People with a series of bad bosses can learn to be like them rather than learning the more desirable lessons in "what not to do." In short, playing people to their strengths requires keeping people doing what they already know how to do. Repeating similar experiences, because they teach negative lessons as well as positives, can enhance and even generate flaws that can, over time, lead to derailment.

If managers stay in the same kinds of assignments with the same kinds of bosses with the same kinds of expectations, then their proven strengths may indeed be sufficient. But in a rapidly changing world such stasis is increasingly difficult to find. A far better strategy than continually seeking out experiences that allow one's strengths to carry them is to seek out the experiences that allow one to develop new strengths.

The need to reconsider strengths is most starkly highlighted in global assignments. When going into foreign cultures, an executive faces multiple challenges and may have to deal with a business situation requiring different strengths as well as with cultural differences that may not welcome behaviors that have worked elsewhere. Repeatedly, in our study of global executives,[26] we heard stories of the need for change as people faced new environments. In case after case after case "old ways won't work" and the need to adapt, to change, and to do things differently was the central theme. We concluded that "the crossing of cultural lines...is an assault on the identity of the person. When the task becomes managing differences of country, culture, language, and values, the assumptions we make about ourselves and other people are brought into question. Effective executive performance when crossing country and cultural borders often demands a kind of transformation of who we are and how we see ourselves."[26]

It is obvious that what worked before (dare we say "strengths") is not sufficient in such contexts. In a separate study of global work, Joyce Osland[29] concluded that crossing cultural boundaries required letting go of "cultural certainty, unquestioned acceptance of basic assumptions, personal frames of reference, the unexamined life, accustomed role and status, knowledge of social reinforcement, accustomed habits and activities, and known routines." If that weren't enough to make one question the efficacy of sticking with strengths, her list of required changes should complete the argument: "positive changes in self, changed attitudes, improved work skills, increased knowledge, and closer family relationships."[29]

Even more recently, Jeff Immelt,[20] CEO of General Electric, addressing an audience consisting primarily of MBAs aspiring to executive careers, said unequivocally that "what counts is your willingness to learn and change." This sentiment is echoed by Mike Lombardo and Bob Eichinger, who reviewed decades of research on leadership development and concluded, "If there is a magic talent that guarantees success, it's recognizing then learning to do what you don't know how to do."[24]

It seems obvious that learning, growth, and change are crucial to success. People are born with certain gifts and develop strengths as they mature that help make them successful at early stages of their lives. Some of these strengths are even a foundation for success later in life. However, the idea that those early strengths are sufficient over time, or that some of them won't become irrelevant or even obstacles to success, is naïve. Nor is it wise to ignore flaws developed early in life because what may not matter much in one setting or life stage can take center stage in another.

Acquisition of Expertise

Research on experts and the acquisition of expertise (e.g. world class musicians, chess grand masters) supports a case for sticking with one's passion but not for staying with all of one's strengths. Unlike non-experts with similar years of experience, experts seek the next challenge rather than staying with their current level of mastery—they "play on the edge."[12,11] In other words, those who become world-class experts are never satisfied with their current level of performance, but, once mastered, seek new approaches that will move them to the next higher level. Tiger Woods, for example, even though he was successful with it, changed his swing several times so that he could get even better.[6]

Simple logic suggests that even those with obvious gifts, such as early demonstration of extraordinary talent in a specific area, cannot progress if they calcify by relying over and over on the same tried and true skill-set. In the world of music, for example, the strengths that make a child prodigy pianist at 5 are not the same as the skills required to be world class at 21. In fact, what leads to success early on can become a habit that must be shed at a later time if one is to reach the next level of expertise. And flaws that might develop at 5 and not matter much can become serious obstacles to growth later on—making yet another case that weaknesses cannot be ignored. Moreover, as if to make the point that has been made over and over, the same research cited above shows that experts, again compared to people with similar years of experience, learn more from their experiences. Rather than relying on what they know, they seek to learn whatever will make them even better—which is another way of saying they are more open to change.

Point-Counter Point

With neither data nor logic supporting the simplistic notion of playing people to their strengths, it's hard to imagine how a case could be made for that approach unless it is argued that 1) this is not applicable to managerial careers; 2) what it really means is that people should build on their strengths (not stick with them), and through that process acquire new ones; 3) what it really means is keeping only *some* strengths, but not all of them. All three options are positive, and avoid trying to fix those pesky flaws. Let's look at them one at a time.

Not everyone aspires to a managerial career; many of those who do are not seeking promotion, and many of those seeking promotions do not deserve them. So we might argue that for the vast majority of people, if not for high potentials, playing to strengths is the best strategy. Unfortunately there is no reason to believe that either non-managers or plateaued managers are immune from changing situations or the ways those changes affect their tapestries of strengths and weaknesses. Nor is living with flaws, even when offset by certain strengths, always the best strategy. Aren't we all familiar with the eventual impact on the morale of a group when jerks are tolerated because they get results or have particular skills that the boss is afraid to lose? Failing to confront the problems erodes confidence in the boss and breeds cynicism in the group.

Another parry is to say that a focus on strengths does not necessarily mean stasis. People can hone the edge on their strengths, continually sharpening them, and can use their strengths to build new strengths, so sticking with strengths does not necessarily mean no change. The problems with this argument are that it can't account for the need to give up certain strengths as required by some transitions, it does not consider that strengths overused can become weaknesses, nor does it acknowledge that different strengths may be required that are not extensions of the existing ones. In terms of the research on expertise, this rationale would produce "performers"—people who reach one level of mastery and stop, satisfied with playing the same tune over and over.

Finally, maybe the initial case was overstated—perhaps the recommendation is not to hang on to *all* strengths, just certain ones. After all, don't some strengths form a foundation that needs to stay in place as one progresses? Even the leadership pipeline perspective[5] includes building a base that supports later progress through the various turns. There is clearly a compelling logic to this argument, but, in addition to not considering the potential harm that flaws can cause, it requires sifting among strengths to identify those to keep and those that don't matter. As the refrain goes in the Kenny Rogers hit, The Gambler, "You've got to know when to hold 'em, know when to fold 'em."

Even if we knew which strengths are crucial to leadership effectiveness in every situation, which we don't, and even if there were only one way to be effective, which there isn't, an overemphasis on selected strengths comes up short. Developing as a leader requires consideration of combinations of strengths and weaknesses, giving up some strengths that have served in the past while simultaneously acquiring new strengths, managing even important and versatile strengths so they aren't turned into weaknesses through overuse, and attending to flaws (sometimes camouflaged as strengths) that, as circumstances change, can cause derailment.

In short, the fallacy is not that strengths are useful, that being positive is more effective than dwelling on the negative, or even that flaws are difficult to change. Rather, the fundamental problem lies in the assumptions underlying those assertions. These include assuming (1) that there are such things as unqualified strengths; (2) that there are flaws that aren't also in some way strengths; (3) that strengths and flaws (if there were clarity about which is which) can be considered independently rather than in combination and in context; (4) that flaws are relatively harmless, either because they can be offset by strengths or have no serious ramifications in the current context; and finally (5) that flaws are always very difficult to correct and so time and effort are better spent on bolstering strengths rather than on trying to fix flaws.

I would argue that each of these assumptions is incorrect or misleading. Every strength is potentially a weakness, either because it is carried to an extreme or because it distracts from what is really needed (for statistical data on this point, see the next chapter by Kaiser & Kaplan).[21] Most "flaws" can be a source of strength as well as a problem, or they were at one time even if in the current context they are not. The complex interplay between strengths and flaws and strategies for capitalizing on the upside while neutralizing the associated downside are discussed in chapter 9 by Malcolm Davies.[8]

Most importantly, strengths and flaws are not only relative and situationally determined, they act in concert, creating complex interactions (tapestries) that offset, enhance, cancel, amplify, and otherwise play out in a given context. The autocrat who listens well, takes input seriously, and creates an environment of success for a team is a different animal than the autocrat who manages people who know more than he/she does but doesn't listen and stifles input. Either of those is different from the autocrat who is truly the expert and doesn't need input to get results.

Some flaws, whether strengths gone awry or simply behaviors that are detrimental in an important situation or across situations, cannot be ignored indefinitely. The derailment research shows clearly that changing situations create malignancies. Nor are all so-called flaws hard to change (although some undeniably are, for a variety of reasons). Sometimes modest improvement is enough; sometimes compensating strategies can be found or new strengths developed that neutralize the problem.

To be sure, for many years too much emphasis has been placed on fixing people, especially in organizations. Coaching, 360 feedback, forced distributions, performance management, and other programs are often applied to fix performance problems, although less exclusively so today than when they were originally introduced. Because of that, an emphasis on strengths is a healthy counteracting trend. But rather than attempting to counteract an over-emphasis on the negative by over-emphasizing the positive, I suggest using the moment to change the game entirely. Dropping the artificial distinction between strengths and weaknesses that has been ingrained by the love affair with competency models, we might more realistically approach developing talent by embracing complexity rather than avoiding it. Following the lead of genetics research,[30] what might happen if we started using language that eschews absolutes? Consider the implications of words and phrases used to describe the various complex interactions that lead to genetic effects, such as emergenic, thresholds, multipliers, triggers, turns on or off, speeds up or slows down, and transient effects.

At the very least such a change in language would allow conversation to explore how things combine to create effects, the circumstances that trigger events and the boundaries and thresholds within which things happen, the situations in which it makes any difference, and how much difference it makes.

The Practitioner's Dilemma

The danger in pushing back against an extreme version of "play people to their strengths" is creating an equally extreme sense that only change is good. Clearly people are not infinitely malleable; nor is it flattering to be seen as inconsistent, wishy-washy, or a dilettante (or, in the never ending political debates, a "flip flopper"). There is value in building a strong foundation, using one's gifts to the fullest, and focusing on what one does well, as well as in adapting to changing situations.

The fact that development is not black and white leaves managers and practitioners in a dilemma. One the one hand, shareholders increasingly emphasize short-term gains, putting increasing pressures on managers to provide them. This leaves managers in a tough situation. The long-term interests of the organization and of the high potential individual are best served by a strategy for developing talent that values diverse experience and increasing competence over time. However, short-term results are most likely achieved by making sure that people are doing what they do well, by avoiding the performance losses that accrue as people climb the learning curve in new situations, and by keeping good people rather than letting them go elsewhere for developmental reasons. Confronting weaknesses in flawed star players also entails risk to short-term results, as they may not respond well to criticism.

Unfortunately, arguments over the relative merits of strengths do little to ease the burden on the person in the trenches. Most savvy practitioners are intuitively aware of the trade-offs involved in developing their people, and of the limited time available to commit to development. But that doesn't change the reality. Developing talent is a leadership issue and there are costs associated with it, just as there are with other business decisions. It may be easier, and in the short-term more effective, to play high potential people to their demonstrated strengths, but the piper eventually will want his pay. Developing leaders with the breadth and experience to handle the complexity of organizations in today's global world simply requires an investment in helping those with talent shed what no longer serves them (both strengths and weaknesses) and continually acquire the new skills that they need.

References

1. Arvey, R., Rotundo, M., Johnson, W., & McGue, M. (2006). The determinants of leadership role occupancy: Genetic and personality factors. *The Leadership Quarterly*, 17, 1-20.

2. Arvey, R. D., Zhang, Z., Avolio, B. J., & Kreuger, R. F. (2007). Developmental and genetic determinants of leadership role occupancy among women. *Journal of Applied Psychology, 92*, 693-706.

3. Berglas, S. (this volume). Victims of their own success.

4. Bridges, W. (1980). *Transitions.* Reading, MA: Addison-Wesley.

5. Charan, R., Drotter, S., & Noel, J. (2001). *The leadership pipeline*. San Francisco: Jossey-Bass.

6. Colvin, (2006, October 30). What it takes to be great. *Fortune*, 88.

7. Coy, P. (2007). Ten years from now. *BusinessWeek Poll*, Retrieved August 20, 2007, from http://www.businessweek.com/magazine/content/07_34/b4047401.htm.

8. Davies, M. R. (this volume). Unlocking the value of exceptional personalities.

9. Dotlich, D., Noel, J., & Walker, N. (2004). *Leadership passages*: *The personal and professional transitions that make or break a leader* San Francisco: John Wiley & Sons.

10. Eliade, M. (1958). *Rites and symbols of initiation*. Putnam, CT.: Spring Publications.

11. Ericcson, K., & Charness, N. (1994). Expert performance: Its structure and acquisition. *American Psychologist, 49*, 727-747.

12. Ericcson, K., Krampe, R., & Tesch-Romer, C. (1993). The role of deliberate practice in the acquisition of expert performance. *Psychological Review, 100*, 363-406.

13. Erikson, E. (1950). *Childhood and society*. New York: Norton.

14. Freedman, A. (2005). Swimming upstream: The challenge of managerial promotions. In R. B. Kaiser (Ed.), *Filling the leadership pipeline*, (pp. 25-44). Greensboro, NC: Center for Creative Leadership.

15. Gabarro, J. (1987). *The dynamics of taking charge*. Boston: Harvard Business School Press.

16. Gilkey, R., & Kilts, C. (2007). Cognitive fitness, *Harvard Business Review*, 85(11), 53-66.

17. Hill, L. (1992). *Becoming a manager*. Boston: Harvard Business School Press.

18. Holmes, S. (2003, December 15). Boeing: What really happened. *BusinessWeek*, 32-48.

19. Howard, A., & Bray, D. (1988). *Managerial lives in transition: Advancing age and changing times*. New York: Guilford.

20. Immelt, J. (2007, November 27) Address at the Marshall School of Business, the University of Southern California, Los Angeles, CA.

21. Kaiser, R. B., & Kaplan, R. E. (this volume). When strengths run amok.

22. Kerstetter, J., & Burrows, P. (2004, July 26). Sun: A CEO's last stand. *BusinessWeek*, 64.

23. Levinson, D. (1978). *The season's of a man's life.* New York: Ballantine.

24. Lombardo M. M., & Eichinger, R. W. (2006). *The leadership machine: Architecture to develop. leaders for any future* (3rd ed.). Minneapolis, MN: Lominger Limited, Inc.

25. McCall, W. M., Jr. (1998). *High flyers.* Boston: Harvard Business School Press.

26. McCall, W. M., Jr., & Hollenbeck, G. (2002). *Developing global executives.* Boston: Harvard Business School Press.

28. McCall, W. M., Jr., & Lombardo, M. (1983). What makes a top executive? *Psychology Today*, 17(2), 26-31.

29. McCall, W. M., Jr., Lombardo, M., & Morrison, A. (1988). *The lessons of experience.* Lexington, MA: Lexington.

30. Osland, J. (1995). *The adventure of working abroad.* San Francisco: Jossey-Bass.

31. Pinker, S. (2002). *The blank slate.* New York: Viking.

32. Saporito, B. (2005, February 21). Why Carly's Out. *Time*, 32.

33. Sengupta, K., Abdel-Hamid, T., & Wassenhove, L. (2008). The experience trap. *Harvard Business Review, 86*(2), 94-101.

34. Van Gennep, A. (1960). *The rites of passage.* Chicago: University of Chicago Press.

CHAPTER 5

WHEN STRENGTHS RUN AMOK

Robert B. Kaiser and Robert E. Kaplan
Kaplan DeVries Inc.

John was known as a "fix-it" manager. His career consisted of one turnaround after another. He had a string of early successes improving non-performing teams then fixing troubled manufacturing plants. Later in his career he turned around a business drowning in red ink. When John was promoted to executive vice president of a profitable division, he was widely admired for his masterful problem solving, deep technical knowledge, and thorough understanding of operations.

But John's tremendous depth came at a tremendous cost: he lacked breadth. John didn't have a broad view of the division and how the different parts fit together. In particular, he did not appreciate staff functions or grasp how to use them to support the business. His network of contacts across the organization was limited. He also did not understand how taking over a profitable business called for him to lead differently from leading a turnaround. It was nine months into his new job and he still felt like a fish out of water, struggling to articulate a strategy for keeping pace as new technologies emerged and fickle customer demand began to change.

John's story is not a corporate anomaly. Everywhere we look, we find managers whose impressive strengths, ironically, contain the seeds of their undoing. In the previous chapter, Morgan McCall[23] provided a conceptual account of the many ways in which "strengths become weaknesses." In this chapter, we elaborate on that idea by providing statistical data on strengths, how few managers know their strengths, how not knowing their strengths makes them liable to overuse them, and how overusing a strength often comes at the expense of opposing but complementary leadership skills and approaches. We also show how these neglected problems with strengths hamper a manager's effectiveness as well as the performance of his or her team. The chapter concludes with solutions for correcting blind spots in the practice of management assessment and development that leave the problems associated with overused strengths undiagnosed.

Most Managers Don't Know their Strengths

The late Peter Drucker constantly advised managers to build on their strengths. However, this seemingly straightforward advice is complicated by his observation that, "Most people think they know what they are good at; they are usually wrong."[7] Recent research in social psychology and on 360-degree feedback shows just how perceptive was this philosopher of modern management.

Competence and Self-Awareness

A 1999 study of competence and self-awareness by two social psychologists at Cornell University, Justin Kruger and David Dunning, caught the attention of the popular press with its clever title, "Unskilled and Unaware." The study compared objective ability to perceived ability in the diverse areas of humor, grammar, and logical reasoning. What the media focused on was the finding that the least skilled individuals grossly over-estimated their abilities. The least skilled estimated their abilities to be well above average despite scoring in the bottom 25% on objective measures. While perhaps humorous to those who have spent time with people who are "too big for their britches," the surprising finding was at the high end of the skill continuum: the people who were most skilled according to objective measures actually rated their own performance closer to average. Follow-up research determined that the most talented individuals held the misguided belief that other people are as capable, or more capable, than they are and that their own ability is not extraordinary.

This general finding that the most talented people tend to underestimate their strengths is consistent with research on 360-degree feedback. Studies comparing self-ratings to coworker ratings find that the most effective managers *underrate* themselves compared to coworkers.[5,9] The strongest performers do not see what they do well as clearly as their coworkers see it. More than a curiosity, these distorted self-perceptions have consequences. Eichinger and Lombardo tracked a cohort of middle managers over time. They found that many of the over-raters' careers had stalled or even derailed, while the under-raters were more likely to get promoted. The researchers concluded that the under-raters were eager learners, open to feedback, set higher standards for themselves, and were never satisfied, constantly seeking self-improvement.

Talented and Unaware

In our work with executives, we find a similar trend. For instance, we compared the self-ratings of over 400 upper-level managers to their coworkers' ratings on the question, "Overall, how effective is this person as a leader on a ten-point scale, where 5 is adequate and 10 is outstanding?" (See Sidebar 1 for a description of the sample.)

Sidebar 1.
Research Sample and Measures

Sample. The research reported in this chapter is based on data for 421 upper-level managers who received 360-degree feedback in either a leadership development program or for executive coaching. One hundred and sixty four of the managers described their organizational level as "Executive," while 257 indicated "General Management." The sample represents over fifteen different companies based in North America and spans several industries (e.g., high-tech, consumer products, financial services, manufacturing, construction, energy). The majority of managers are male (79%).

In addition to self-assessments, ratings were also collected from a total of 4,202 coworkers—621 superiors, 1,680 peers, and 1,901 subordinates. Typically, each manager was rated by one or two superiors, four peers, and four or five subordinates.

To simplify interpretation of the results, all analyses were based on either self-ratings or the average rating computed across all coworkers for a given individual.

Measures. Three survey-based measures of leadership effectiveness were used. Each measure was rated by the focal manager as well as his or her coworkers.

1. *Overall effectiveness* was measured with the question, "Please rate this person's overall effectiveness as a leader on a ten-point scale where 5 is a*dequate* and 10 is *outstanding.*" Prior research has demonstrated that this single-item rating is reliable and correlates highly with multi-item scales that measure the perceived effectiveness of individual leaders.[13]

(Sidebar Continues)

Sidebar 1. (cont.)

2. *Team vitality* reflects the favorability of the attitudes collectively held by the subordinates of each manager. This scale contains three items concerning morale, engagement, and cohesiveness that are rated on a five-point scale where higher ratings indicate more favorable attitudes. The internal consistency reliability (coefficient alpha) of this scale in the present sample was .83.

3. *Team productivity* reflects the productivity level of the team that reports to each manager. This scale contains three items concerning quantity, quality, and overall output that are rated on a 5-point scale where higher ratings indicate more of the attribute in question. The internal consistency reliability (coefficient alpha) of this scale was .84.

Measures of effectiveness were not available for all managers in the sample. *Overall effectiveness* ratings were available for 411 of the 421 total managers. *Team vitality* and *team productivity* ratings were only available for 152 managers (all of whom were self-identified as at the "Executive" level).

Leader behavior was measured with the *Leadership Versatility Index®* (*LVI*) 360-degree feedback instrument,[13,18] which is described in the text under the heading, *Measuring Overused Strengths*. All 421 managers in the sample were rated on the *LVI*.

Using coworker ratings to classify the managers by quartiles ranging from *least effective* to *most effective*, the average self- and coworker rating of overall effectiveness for each quartile is presented in Figure 1. In the bottom quartile, the least effective managers tended to overrate their effectiveness. But in the top quartile, the most effective managers underrated their effectiveness, and by a wide margin. Despite being regarded by others as highly effective, they viewed their own performance as about average.

Through assessment-and-development consulting to individual executives, we have found that they often do not know the extent of their own strengths—especially the outstanding ones—and, ironically, they are uncomfortable with feedback about their strengths.[15,18] When confronted with information that highlights the discrepancy between their self-view and coworker views (and even objective data), they are at no loss for discounting the praise. There are many reasons why executives resist positive feedback.[19] For one, there is the common discomfort with compliments. Most people find it mildly embarrassing to receive praise. Some worry about becoming complacent. Others fear becoming arrogant by letting the positives go to their heads. Strong norms against bragging are also at play. So is the well-documented "negativity bias"—the evolutionary-based tendency to place greater attention on threats than on rewards because threats were more central to the survival of our ancestors.[2,27]

Figure 1.
Talented and Unaware: Comparing Self-Ratings and Coworker Ratings of Overall Effectiveness

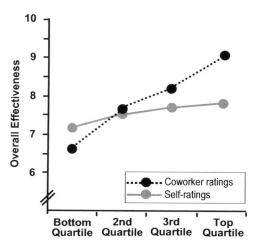

Note: Based on ratings for 411 upper-level managers to the item, "Please rate this leader's overall effectiveness on a scale from 1 to 10, where 5 is adequate and 10 is outstanding." The figure shows how managers rated by coworkers in the bottom quartile on overall effectiveness tend to overrate their effectiveness, while managers rated by coworkers in the top quartile tend to underrate their effectiveness.

Strengths Overused

When managers underestimate their strengths, it can have a corrupting effect on their performance. Not knowing their strengths, managers are liable to overuse them. This is one way in which strengths become weaknesses.

McCall and Lombardo's[24] original interview studies at the Center for Creative Leadership of derailed executives introduced the phrase "strengths can become weaknesses." However, little quantitative research has examined this problem. One reason is because hardly any measures of leadership behavior are designed to pick up when managers go overboard; most measures are based on rating scales with response options ranging from 1 to 5 with the underlying assumption that "more is better."[12] However, one exception is the *Leadership Versatility Index*® (*LVI*) 360-degree feedback instrument.

Measuring Overused Strengths

We designed the *Leadership Versatility Index*® on the premise that there are two types of performance problems: shortcomings—when managers display too little of an important leadership behavior—and strengths overused—when managers apply a particular behavior too much or with too much intensity.[12,18] The new rating scale we developed for the *LVI* ranges from -4 to +4, where values between -4 and -1 represent degrees of doing *too little*, 0 represents doing *the right amount*, and values from +1 to +4 represent degrees of doing *too much* (see Figure 2).

Figure 2.
The Too Little/Too Much Rating Scale

Note that this rating scale is probably different from scales that you are accustomed to using. On this scale the best score is "0," in the middle of the scale. The premise is that performance problems arise when managers either do too little or do too much of something.

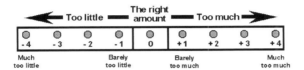

WARNING: Some people misread this scale. Please do not mistake it for one where higher scores are better.

Note: Reproduced from Kaiser, R.B. and Kaplan, R.E. (2007), *Leadership Versatility Index®: Facilitator's Guide*. Greensboro, NC: Kaplan Devries, Inc. Reprinted with permission. The method of assessment used by the *LVI* is protected by U.S. Patent No. 7,121,830.

The *too little/too much* rating scale is applied to 48 specific behavioral items that measure four aspects of leadership with 12 items each. The four dimensions are labeled *Forceful*, *Enabling*, *Strategic*, and *Operational*. Forceful leadership is defined as exercising power and authority to push for performance and includes taking charge, being decisive, and holding people accountable. Enabling leadership is defined as creating conditions for other people to contribute and includes empowerment, participation, and providing support. Strategic leadership is defined as positioning the organization to be competitive in the future and includes setting direction, growing capability, and supporting innovation. Finally, Operational leadership is defined as focusing the organization to get results in the near term and includes managing the day-to-day details of implementation, conserving resources, and establishing an orderly flow of work.

Table 1 presents the means, standard deviations, and the percentages of managers in the present sample rated as doing *too little*, *the right amount*, and *too much* on the Forceful, Enabling, Strategic, and Operational dimensions.

Overkill is Everywhere

As shown in Table 1, managers do in fact overdo each of the four broad dimensions of leadership. Specifically, 38% of managers in the present sample were rated as doing *too much* Forceful leadership, 12% as doing *too much* Enabling leadership, only 4% as doing *too much* Strategic leadership, and 11% as doing *too much* operational leadership. Our analysis of the results for individual managers found that over half (55%) were rated as doing *too much* on at least one of the four dimensions.

Table 1.
Means, Standard Deviations, and Proportion of Managers Rated As Doing Too Little, the Right Amount, and Too Much on the LVI Scales

	Mean	SD	Too little	The right amount	Too much
Forceful	-.06	.51	54%	9%	38%
Enabling	-.36	.42	78%	10%	12%
Strategic	-.44	.34	91%	5%	4%
Operational	-.19	.23	72%	16%	11%

Note: Based on ratings averaged across all coworkers. *N* = 421 upper-level managers.

Moving from the four broad dimensions to the 48 specific behavioral items, the incidence of overdoing appears even more widespread. Every single manager in the sample was rated as doing *too much* of at least one specific behavior. Ninety-four percent of the sample was rated as doing *too much* of five or more specific behaviors. Over half of the sample was rated as doing *too much* of 10 or more specific behaviors. In other words, the problem of overused strengths is real and pervasive, applying to all managers to some degree and to most managers to a large degree.

Overdoing and Unaware

We next examined the extent to which managers prone to overdoing Forceful, Enabling, Strategic, and Operational leadership recognized this tendency. Of the managers rated by coworkers as doing *too much* Forceful or Strategic leadership, nearly two-thirds also rated themselves as doing *too much* (64% for Forceful and 65% for Strategic). However, a minority of the managers rated by coworkers as doing *too much* Enabling or Operational leadership also rated themselves as doing *too much* (40% on Enabling, 28% on Operational).

Less than half (47%) of the individuals rated as overdoing it by coworkers on one or more of the four dimensions also rated themselves as overdoing those dimensions. The majority of managers who overuse their strengths evidently do not recognize their tendency to go overboard.

Carried Away by What Comes Easily

Many professionals who use the *LVI* in executive coaching or as the feedback component in leadership development programs also use a strengths inventory, such as *Values in Action* (*VIA*)[25] or the *Clifton StrengthsFinder.*[4] Managers complete a strengths inventory to identify their areas of natural-born talent, ability, and interest, and their coworkers provide feedback on the *LVI* to identify how they use those talents, abilities, and interests.

A common finding is that managers tend to overdo behaviors related to their areas of talent—the bigger their hammer, the more every thing looks like a nail. Consider a senior manager who received his "top five signature themes" or greatest areas of talent on the *Clifton StrengthsFinder*. His top five were "Self-assurance" (confidence and poise), "Activator" (urgency about results), "Achiever" (stamina and hard work), "Focus" (staying on task), and "Command" (controlling and decisive). The coworker feedback on the *LVI* revealed a tendency to be too forceful in his approach and too operational in his focus. This is not surprising: managers tend to engage in behaviors that come easily to them because of innate talent; however, not being aware of these talents, they are likely to overuse them.

The Costs of Strengths Overused

It is one thing to document the tendency for managers to overdo behaviors related to their areas of natural-born talent and inclination. It is another matter to determine the impact of going overboard. Using the present sample, we studied the relationship between overdoing Forceful, Enabling, Strategic, and Operational leadership and ratings of the individual's overall effectiveness as a leader, as well as the performance of his or her team. In all cases, the direct cost of overkill is diminished effectiveness. The *hidden* costs of overkill are equally detrimental, if less immediately obvious.

Overdoing is Ineffective

Figure 3 shows the curvilinear relationships between ratings on the four dimensions of leadership behavior and overall effectiveness. For each dimension of behavior the relationship is an inverted-U function, with the highest levels of effectiveness associated with behaviors rated near 0 (*the right amount*). The more a manager is rated as doing *too much* of each dimension, the lower that manager's rating of overall effectiveness. Moreover, doing *too much* of each dimension is just as deleterious to effectiveness as is doing *too little*.

A similar pattern is evident in the relationships between Forceful, Enabling, Strategic, and Operational leadership and the two measures of the performance of the manager's team, team vitality and team productivity. Team vitality refers to how team members feel about the work and each other and is measured by morale, engagement, and cohesion. Team productivity represents the results-oriented aspect of team performance and is measured in terms of quantity, quality, and overall output.

Figure 4 shows the curvilinear relationships between ratings on the four dimensions of leadership and team vitality and productivity. Again, the figures show how doing too much of each leadership dimension is associated with lower team performance, just as is doing too little of each dimension. It is interesting to note that overdoing Forceful leadership has a stronger depressing effect on team vitality while overdoing Enabling leadership has a stronger depressing effect on team productivity. Managers who are too tough and aggressive make employees feel worse about the work and each other while managers who are too inclusive and concerned about people have teams that get softer results.

Strengths overused clearly have negative consequences: doing too much of essential leadership behaviors diminishes a manager's perceived effectiveness and degrades the performance of his or her team.

Figure 3.
Overall Effectiveness as a Function of Forceful, Enabling, Strategic, and Operational Leadership

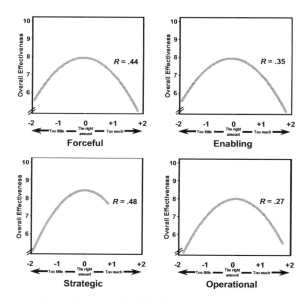

Note: Based on average All Coworker ratings for N = 411 upper-level managers. Curve functions and multiple correlations (R values) are based on quadratic regression analyses. Model statistics are as follows: Forceful $F(2, 408)$ = 48.38, $p < .001$; Enabling $F(2, 408)$ = 28.63, $p < .001$; Strategic $F(2, 408)$ = 61.76, $p < .001$; Operational $F(2, 408)$ = 16.19, $p < .001$.

These findings call into question some applications derived from positive psychology and strengths-based development. Proponents of strengths-based development often hold a "more is better" assumption about strengths; some even deny that one could overdo a strength.[3] One popular intervention has people identify their strengths and then find new ways to apply those strengths.[28] The problem is that this advice can encourage managers to indiscriminately apply their strengths. But when applied at the wrong time and to the wrong degree, overused strengths can cause serious problems for individual careers and the performance of teams and organizations. Furthermore, focusing on the strengths that come naturally begs questions about what doesn't come so naturally.

As if the direct costs of strengths overused were not harmful enough, there are also hidden costs. In particular, overused strengths crowd out the other side. For instance, managers prone to deciding too quickly often neglect to involve people in the decision-making process. This results in what we refer to as "lopsided leadership."[17,18]

Figure 4.
Team Performance as a Function of Forceful, Enabling, Strategic, and Operational Leadership

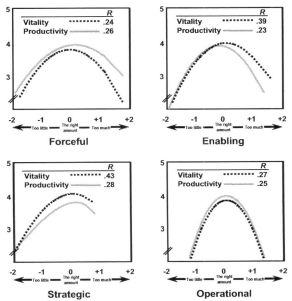

Note: Based on average All Coworker ratings for $N = 152$ executives. Curve functions and multiple correlations (R values) are based on quadratic regression analyses. Black dotted lines represent relationships with Team Vitality; solid gray lines represent relationships with Team Productivity. Model statistics are as follows: Forceful and Vitality $F(2, 149) = 4.53$, $p < .05$; Forceful and Productivity $F(2, 149) = 5.18$, $p < .01$; Enabling and Vitality $F(2, 149) = 13.57$, $p < .001$; Enabling and Productivity $F(2, 149) = 3.99$, $p < .05$; Strategic and Vitality $F(2, 149) = 16.89$, $p < .001$; Strategic and Productivity $F(2, 149) = 6.33$, $p < .01$; Operational and Vitality $F(2, 149) = 5.98$, $p < .01$; Operational and Productivity $F(2, 149) = 5.12$, $p < .01$. The curves for the Strategic dimension only extend to the +1 range because no one in the sample was rated higher than that value.

Lopsided Leadership

Leadership theorists regularly define the role requirements and behavioral dimensions of leadership in terms of "yin-yang" pairs of opposites—autocratic versus democratic, task-oriented versus people-oriented, initiative versus consideration, internally focused versus externally focused, transactional versus transformational, and so on. These distinctions are represented in the behavioral model covered by the *LVI*. Forceful and Enabling leadership comprise the yin-yang pair of dimensions concerning a leader's interpersonal style, or *how* one leads. Strategic and Operational leadership comprise the yin-yang pair of dimensions concerning organizational substance, or *what* one leads.[14,18]

Rare is the manager who makes appropriate use of both sides of the Forceful-Enabling pair and the Strategic-Operational pair. Instead, most managers are lopsided—they lean one way by doing too much of one approach while simultaneously doing too little of the opposing, complementary approach. In the present sample, we found that overdoing one dimension nearly guaranteed that a manager underdoes the opposite dimension. Among the managers who were rated as doing *too much* Forceful leadership, 97% were also rated as doing *too little* Enabling. Of those rated as *too much* Enabling, 86% were rated as *too little* Forceful. The same pattern is evident for the other duality: among the few managers rated as emphasizing Strategic leadership *too much*, 67% were also rated as *too little* Operational. And of those who were rated as too Operational, 94% were rated as not Strategic enough.

Lopsided leadership is the second way in which strengths become weaknesses. By overemphasizing one approach, managers neglect the complementary approach. Interestingly, this tendency was discovered in the early research on derailment, but did not seem to register in the collective mentality of the leadership development field. For instance, McCall and Lombardo[24] reported accounts of derailed managers who were brilliant technical problem solvers but were short on people skills, micro-managers who got so bogged down in operational detail that they couldn't think strategically, and so forth. Lopsided leadership is a rampant, if under-appreciated, problem, rooted in the all-too-human tendency to over-idealize what comes naturally and to devalue what doesn't come so naturally.[17] By identifying so powerfully with one side, lopsided leaders turn their backs on the other side, and it becomes their blind side.

Neglecting What Doesn't Come Easily

Earlier, we described how managers tend to overdo behaviors related to their innate talents. This may not surprise those with experience in management development. However, there is also a less obvious side effect: managers tend to neglect, or *underdo*, opposing but complementary behaviors. This principal is illustrated by the manager who learned from a strengths inventory that his top five areas of talent were Self-assurance, Activator, Achiever, Focus, and Command. While his *LVI* feedback indicated a tendency to be too forceful and operational, it also revealed an even stronger tendency to not be enabling and strategic enough.

This example is typical. Overdoing behaviors related to one's talent is common, and so is avoiding opposing skills and behaviors. In fact, the tendency to underdo what doesn't come naturally may be stronger than the tendency to overdo what does. It is probably a function of how people form their self-concept and the tendency to disparage what they define as "not me." As Peter Drucker put it,[7] "Far too many people—especially people with great expertise in one area—are contemptuous of knowledge in other areas." It is little wonder that many upper-level managers are lopsided.

The High Value of Versatility

Lopsided leadership may be the single most important developmental need among upper-level managers. Therefore, our approach to development involves toning down overused strengths and building capability with complementary, but underdeveloped, skills. The ultimate goal for lopsided leaders is versatility, a full range of motion defined by capability with opposing approaches, unlimited by a bias in favor of one and prejudice against the other.[16,17,18] We emphasize the idea of versatility as a mastery of opposites because this integrative, higher-order concept distinguishes the best managers from the rest.

We can quantify how versatile managers are in terms of a pair like Forceful and Enabling leadership by calculating how close their ratings are to *the right amount* on both dimensions. These scores can be expressed as a percentage, where 100% indicates perfect versatility (doing the right amount of every pair of behaviors) and lower percentages indicate doing too much of some and too little of other behaviors.[*] We calculate separate Versatility Scores for Forceful-Enabling leadership and Strategic-Operational leadership, and then take the average of the two to arrive at an Overall Versatility Score.

Making the Grade

Figure 5 presents the distribution of Overall Versatility Scores for the present sample of 421 upper-level managers. The distribution looks remarkably like distributions for school grades, with an average of 81% and standard deviation of 7%.

We interpret Versatility Scores like letter grades—90% and up, A; 80-90%, B; 70-80%, C, and so on. By this standard, the majority of managers get "*B*s" in terms of versatility (57.1%). Very few managers get lower than a "*D*" (1%). And just over 1 in 20 managers get "*A*s" (5.7%). Granted, the *LVI* does not grade on a curve; nonetheless, this low incidence of versatile managers is consistent with other studies based on different measures and different methodologies that also find only a small minority of managers to be agile, balanced, or otherwise well-rounded.[22,29]

Versatility and Effective Leadership

Versatility may be the master competency among the competencies that Eichinger, Dai, and Tang[8] referred to as *distinctively competitive and aligned*. That is, few managers are truly versatile, yet versatility is highly related to effectiveness. Versatility as measured by the *LVI* is correlated with subordinate job satisfaction, commitment, and desire to quit; with team morale, engagement, and cohesion; with unit productivity; and with ratings of overall leadership effectiveness.[13]

In the present sample, coworker ratings of overall versatility were correlated with ratings of overall effectiveness ($r = .61$) among the 411 upper-level managers for whom we had effectiveness ratings. In the subsample of 152 executives for whom we had measures of team performance, coworker ratings of overall versatility were correlated with both team vitality ($r = .65$) and team productivity ($r = .41$).

Lower the Bar?

Some may argue, as some proponents of strengths-based development do, that it is not reasonable to expect managers to be well-rounded, jacks-of-all-trades. After all, even the current research suggests that only 1 in 20 managers is versatile, capable with opposing skill-sets like Forceful and Enabling or Strategic and Operational. The extreme version of the argument denies that strengths can be overused altogether and suggests that trying to get better in an area of weakness is a misallocation of time, energy, and money because the better return is in maximizing strengths.[3,4]

---

[*]For the details on the computation of Versatility Scores, see the appendix in *The Versatile Leader: Make the Most of Your Strengths— Without Overdoing It* [18] or *Leadership Versatility Index® Facilitator's Guide*.[13]

Figure 5.
Distribution of Overall Versatility Scores

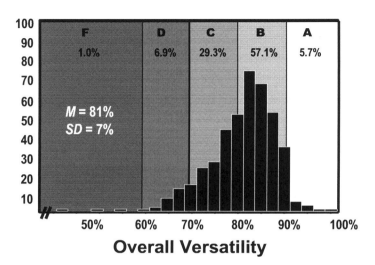

Note: Based on average All Coworker ratings for *N* = 421 upper-level managers. Versatility scores can be interpreted like letter grades in school (90-100% *A*, 80-90% *B*, 70-80% *C* and so on). The percentages in the top of each color-coded "grade band" indicate the percentage of the managers in the sample who scored in that range.

It is true that versatile leaders are rare. It may be the case that not every manager can become a truly versatile leader. At the same time, versatility is not an all-or-none proposition; most managers can become more versatile to some degree by toning down what they do too much and ramping up what they do too little. These adjustments increase versatility, which corresponds to increased perceived effectiveness and team performance. Ultimate versatility may be elusive for most, but improvement is possible for all and likely to pay off for the individual and the organization.

A recent *Harvard Business Review* article suggested that it is time to end "the myth of the complete leader (and the attendant fear of appearing incompetent)" and focus instead on maximizing strengths and collaborating with individuals who have complementary strengths.[1] However, little attention was paid to the difficulties of establishing trust and respect despite major differences in skills, perspectives, and values that are so common on diverse terms. Moreover, in the wake of a rash of corporate scandals, public debate over outsized executive compensation, and a meltdown in the global economy due to corporate greed and a lack of prudent oversight, we don't need to be lowering expectations for senior managers; we need to be raising them.

Implications

Building on the recognition that most managers do not know their strengths, we have demonstrated that most managers overuse their strengths. Strengths overused cause two problems: first, doing too much of key leadership behaviors is just as ineffective as is doing too little of those behaviors. Second, overdoing one approach is linked with underdoing an opposing yet complementary approach, which further diminishes effectiveness. Moreover, versatile managers who demonstrate a mastery of opposing leadership approaches are uncommon. Nonetheless, most managers can become more versatile by doing less of what they overdo and by doing more of what they underdo, and increased versatility is associated with higher levels of leadership effectiveness and team performance.

The practical implications that flow logically from these statistical findings and our point of view on leadership are relevant to how one uses strengths-based development. On the one hand, this chapter indicates that a successful philosophy of strengths-based development must consider the related problems of overused strengths and lopsided leadership. On the other hand, an enlightened approach to strengths-based development requires changes in the standard practice of managerial assessment to detect overused strengths and lopsidedness.

Applications

The cornerstone to leadership development is self-awareness.[11] In particular, two types of self-awareness are needed: one, insight into one's strengths (and liabilities) and two, an understanding of how one uses those strengths. This distinction suggests two complementary types of assessment to guide development.

Discover your strengths. The first type of assessment needs to help an individual identify her strengths. Those are likely to be in areas of natural-born talent, which can be determined by identifying the types of activities one is drawn to, enjoys doing, and for which one has aptitude.[4] Several "strengths inventories" are available for this purpose, including *Values in Action (VIA)*[25] and the revamped *StrengthsFinder 2.0.*[26] These inventories ask respondents to identify the activities they enjoy, prefer, and succeed at to determine a rank-ordering of the most to least prominent areas of talent.

Standard temperament and personality inventories are another method of identifying a manager's natural inclinations, talents, and areas of strength. One benefit of omnibus personality assessment tools is that they offer comparative feedback to calibrate where one stands relative to an appropriate norm group. Strengths inventories like *StrengthsFinder 2.0* only provide a rank order of one's most prominent areas of talent, or one's "personal best" strengths. They do not provide comparisons to a normative sample, thus precluding the identification of what Eichinger, Dai, and Tang referred to in chapter 2 as "competitive" strengths, "distinctively competitive" strengths, and "distinctively competitive and aligned" strengths. Further, some personality test batteries—like those discussed in chapter 8[11] and chapter 9[6]—include assessments of both "bright side" characteristics (strengths) and "dark side" characteristics (weaknesses), thus providing a more balanced picture of the person.

A little-recognized obstacle stands in the way of helping managers embrace their strengths. The resistance starts with, of all things, a bad attitude about good news. Many leaders are impatient with affirmation, which they regard as a feel-good experience. To them it is the criticism that's truly useful. "Let's move on to the negatives, that's what I can do something about," goes the mentality. A related problem managers face in coming to know their strengths is trouble accepting affirmation once you get them to consider it. For a host of reasons, leaders actually resist changing their minds about their strengths.[15] It is often not enough to review the results of a self-assessment on a strengths inventory for a manager to truly get the message. Therefore, while there is developmental value in the affirmation provided by a strengths assessment, leaders need help paying attention to it and then taking it in, the necessary steps prior to putting their talent to better use. (For strategies for contending with resistance to positive feedback, see Kaplan & Kaiser).[19]

Discover how you use your strengths. When debriefed by a skilled facilitator, strengths inventories and personality assessments can raise awareness about strengths. But these assessments do not say anything about how a manager deploys those strengths. This type of assessment requires coworker feedback. However, the typical 360-degree survey is ill-equipped to provide the type of feedback needed to identify strengths overused or lopsided leadership.

Managers rarely get clear feedback about overused strengths. Feedback surveys with a typical 5-point response scale are designed on the tacit assumption that more is better, since high scores are considered better.[21] These types of ratings do not distinguish when managers do something a lot from when they do it too much and therefore confuse activity and effectiveness. And rating scales that ask the respondent to evaluate how effective a manager is with a given behavior do not separate doing too little and doing too much as distinct sources of ineffectiveness. In both cases, managers are deprived of clear feedback about strengths overused.[12]

There are two solutions for helping managers gain awareness about overused strengths. First, recipients of feedback in the form of ratings on 1-to-5 "more is better" scales can clarify if high scores may mask a tendency to overdo it by following up with coworkers and explicitly asking if they tend to overdo those behaviors. The ensuing conversation can be beneficial for both parties. The second, more involved, solution is to replace assessment scoring systems built on the conception of "strengths and weaknesses" with scoring systems designed on the tripartite view of "shortcomings, strengths, and strengths overused."[18] For instance, global assessments of a manager's performance can ask respondents to indicate which behaviors, skills, and competencies fit into each of the three categories. This type of assessment is similar to Peter Drucker's advice to ask coworkers, "What should I start doing (shortcomings), keep doing (strengths), and stop doing (strengths overused) to be more effective?"

But the expanded view of assessment in terms of shortcomings, strengths, and strengths overused is not enough to identify lopsided leadership. This is because most competency models and 360-degree feedback tools are based on conceptual models of leadership that simply lay out the dimensions and behaviors one at a time. They have the design elegance of a shopping list. What is missing in these models is the dynamic relationship among the various dimensions, the tensions and trade-offs that make management a balancing act.

Lopsidedness is by definition a two-sided concept—too much of this, too little of that. For 360-degree feedback tools to reveal lopsidedness, they need to be based on a model of leadership constructed in terms of pairs of opposites, like yin and yang. Two major pairs of opposites that any competent leadership assessment must cover concern interpersonal style (e.g., Forceful versus Enabling) and organizational substance (e.g., Strategic versus Operational).

Measured Enthusiasm

Prescriptions like "play to your strengths" and "build on the positives" are often offered as a simple solution to the complex problem of management development. But we should be leery of the slippery slope leading from simple to simplistic. There is a grain of truth to these prescriptions, but there is also more to the story.

Emphasizing a focus on strengths without recognition of the problem of strengths overused can encourage managers to go overboard, become lopsided, and hamper performance. Further, a focus on strengths to the neglect of addressing weaknesses misses a key point: leadership roles are not elective, and if a manager does not perform some roles because they do not play to his strengths, then both the manager's effectiveness and the performance of his team will suffer.

References

1. Ancona, D., Malone, T., Orlikowski, N., & Senge, P. (2007). In praise of the incomplete leader. *Harvard Business Review, 85*(2), 92-100.

2. Baumeister, R., Bratslavsky, E., Finkenauer, C., & Vohs, K. (2001). Bad is stronger than good. *Review of General Psychology, 5*, 323-70.

3. Brim, B. (2007, February 8). Probing the dark side of employees' strengths. *Gallup Management Journal*. Retrieved February 15, 2007, from *http://gmj.gallup.com*.

4. Buckingham, M., & Clifton, D. O. (2001). *Now, discover your strengths*. New York: Free Press.

5. Church, A. H. (1997). Managerial self-awareness in high-performing individuals in organizations. *Journal of Applied Psychology, 82*, 281-292.

6. Davies, M. R. (this volume). Unlocking the value of exceptional personalities.

7. Drucker, P. F. (1999). Managing oneself. *Harvard Business Review, 83*(1), 100-109.

8. Eichinger, R. W., Dai, G., & Tang, K. Y. (this volume). It depends upon what you mean by a strength.

9. Eichinger, R. W., & Lombardo, M. M. (2003). Knowledge Summary Series: 360-degree assessment. *Human Resources Planning, 26*(4), 34-44.

10. Gentry, W. A. & Chappellow, C. T. (this volume). Managerial derailment: Weaknesses that can be fixed.

11. Hogan, R., & Benson, M. J. (this volume). Personality theory and positive psychology: Strategic self-awareness.

12. Kaiser, R. B., & Kaplan, R. E. (2005). Overlooking overkill? Beyond the 1-to-5 rating scale. *Human Resources Planning, 28*(3), 7-11.

13. Kaiser, R. B., & Kaplan, R. E. (2007). *Leadership Versatility Index® facilitator's guide*. Greensboro, NC: Kaplan DeVries Inc.

14. Kaiser, R. B., Lindberg, J. T., & Craig, S. B. (2007). Assessing the flexibility of managers: A comparison of methods. *International Journal of Selection and Assessment, 16*, 40-55.

15. Kaplan, R. E. (1999). *Internalizing strengths: An overlooked way of overcoming weaknesses in managers*. Greensboro, NC: Center for Creative Leadership.

16. Kaplan, R. E., & Kaiser, R. B. (2003a). Developing versatile leadership. *MIT Sloan Management Review, 44*(4), 19-26.

17. Kaplan, R. E., & Kaiser, R. B. (2003b). Rethinking a classic distinction in leadership: Implications for the assessment and development of executives. *Consulting Psychology Journal: Practice and Research, 55*, 15-25.

18. Kaplan, R. E., & Kaiser, R. B. (2006). *The versatile leader: Make the most of your strengths—without overdoing it*. San Francisco: Pfeiffer.

19.   Kaplan, R. E., & Kaiser, R. B. (in press). Towards a positive psychology for leaders. In P. A. Linley, S. Harrington, & N. Page (Eds.), *Oxford Handbook of Positive Psychology and Work*. New York: Oxford University Press.

20.   Kruger, J., & Dunning, D. (1999). Unskilled and unaware of it: How difficulties in recognizing one's own incompetence lead to inflated self-assessments. *Journal of Personality and Social Psychology, 77*, 1121-1134.

21.   Leslie, J. B., & Fleenor, J. W. (1998). *Feedback to managers: A review and comparison of multi-rater instruments for management development*. Greensboro, NC: Center for Creative Leadership.

22.   Lombardo, M. M., & Eichinger, R. W. (2000). *The leadership machine*. Minneapolis, MN: Lominger Limited, Inc.

23.   McCall, M. W., Jr. (this volume). Every strength a weakness and other caveats.

24.   McCall, M. W. Jr., & Lombardo, M. M. (1983). *Off the track: Why and how successful executives get derailed.* Technical Report No. 21. Greensboro, NC: Center for Creative Leadership.

25.   Peterson, C., & Seligman, M. E. P. (2002). *The VIA classification of strengths.* Cincinnati, OH: Values in Action Institute.

26.   Rath, T. (2005). *Strengths Finder 2.0*. New York: Gallup Press.

27.   Rozin, P., & Royzman, E. B. (2001). Negativity bias, negativity dominance, and contagion. *Personality and Social Psychology Review, 5*, 296-320.

28.   Seligman, M. E. P., Steen, T. A., Park, N., & Peterson, C. (2005). Positive psychology progress. *American Psychologist, 60*, 410-421.

29.   Wilson, C. L. (2003). *How and why effective managers balance their skills*. Boulder, CO: Clark Wilson Group.

CHAPTER 6

VICTIMS OF THEIR OWN SUCCESS

Steven Berglas, Ph.D.
The Harold and Pauline Price Center for Entrepreneurial Studies
UCLA Anderson School of Management

Faith is believing what you know ain't so.
— Mark Twain

Few executives have the skill and acumen to achieve authentic career success. By authentic career success I mean rising to the top of a demanding corporate hierarchy on the basis of talent and hard work. Those who succeed in this manner do so, as the old Smith Barney advertisement went, "the old fashioned way...they *earn* it." The notion of hard-won success is a powerful image in our collective consciousness. Pilgrims, pioneers in Conestoga wagons, astronauts—these people *earned* success and, according to our cultural iconology, should be on top of the world in terms of material wealth and personal satisfaction.

In my consulting and coaching work with executives, however, I have found that although most who achieve success the old-fashioned way are wealthy, many are not personally satisfied or psychologically at ease; roughly 25% actually become victims of their own success.[7] Since none of the executives I have analyzed had attributes predisposing them to self-destruct (e.g. psychological disorders, biochemical imbalances, etc.), it raises the question, "Why, after achieving the American Dream, do so many people fail to thrive?"

In this chapter, I explore how accentuating the positive can indeed lead to success but once attained, success may be neither lasting nor personally fulfilling. This perspective touches on themes discussed in other chapters in this book—for instance, how success can go to one's head, how strengths can become weaknesses, and how weaknesses that may not have mattered in the past can prove to be one's undoing when circumstances change. However, my goal is to introduce and focus on the idea that the very nature of success and its cultural significance change the way successful people view themselves. I also explain how this change in self-perception is the key to understanding how success can sow the seeds of discontent and foreshadow eventual failure.

America's Most Successful Entrepreneur

When I lecture to groups of executives or teach MBA classes and mention the name Ken Olsen, I get that deer-in-the-headlights reaction every speaker loathes. This would not have been the case 20 years ago. The October 27, 1986 cover story in FORTUNE magazine declared Ken Olsen "America's Most Successful Entrepreneur." This accolade was not just more business press hype. Not only had Olsen's Digital Equipment Corporation (DEC) changed the way people used computers, but also in the 29 years since Olsen had cofounded the company with his *MIT* schoolmate, Harlan Anderson, DEC had gone from a bright idea to $7.6 billion in annual revenues. When FORTUNE honored Olsen, DEC was bigger than Ford Motor Co. was when Henry Ford died, bigger than U.S. Steel when Andrew Carnegie sold out, and bigger than Standard Oil when John D. Rockefeller departed.

As a result of his entrepreneurial climb from lab to riches, Olsen seemed to have secured an impenetrable industry niche for DEC. But as anyone in business knows, "impenetrable niche" is an oxymoron, particularly in the IT industry. In 1992, a mere 6 years after being put on a pedestal by FORTUNE, Olsen was knocked off in ignoble fashion: He was blamed for putting DEC into more than $2 billion of debt, and his resignation soon followed.

No one assumes that Ken Olsen suddenly went mad after being named America's most successful entrepreneur. Actually, few people assume that there was any causal connection between Olsen's success and his subsequent demise. There was a connection, but its pernicious effect began operating long before the public acclaim.

The Technobumpkin

While CEO of DEC, Ken Olsen stayed grounded in his engineering roots, preferring to avoid the limelight commonly commanded by CEOs. The FORTUNE article noted that Olsen's passport stated that his occupation was engineer rather than CEO. True to his engineering personality, Olsen was notorious for spending hours sweating the details of DEC's computers, hanging out with engineers, and making sure, for example, that plugs and connectors were neatly laid out on the backs of DEC's products.

The stamp Olsen put on DEC was one that would make an engineer proud: superior technology and product development, in contrast, for example, to IBM under Thomas Watson Sr., who made Big Blue an aggressive, super-competitive organization that emphasized selling above all else. For this reason, Olsen was called a "technobumpkin" by his lieutenants, a term used in a teasingly affectionate way by some, but also derisively by others.

The frequency with which those in Olsen's inner circle began calling him technobumpkin with contempt began to rise soon after DEC appeared to be on top of the world. In 1965 Olsen launched the PDP-8, the first mass-produced minicomputer. He then refined it, launching the PDP-11 in 1970. Amazingly, the PDP-11 sold so well it was not discontinued until 1997. Yet despite the wild success of the PDP-11, as early as 1972 many of DEC's engineers were pushing Olsen to make a personal computer, like the desktop models being developed in Silicon Valley. Olsen was dead-set against the idea. In one of the most infamous business quotations of all time, Olsen stated at the 1977 World Future Society meeting in Boston, "There is no reason for any individual to have a computer in their [sic] home." Even after DEC engineers analyzed and had a chance to adapt *Apple II*, and then lobbied to get Olsen to embrace the revolution they saw coming, he dismissed them thusly: "They make toys out there in Silicon Valley." The company soon started hemorrhaging red ink, and the rest, as they say, is history.

Was Hubris the Culprit?

Most people feel they know Ken Olsen-type executives: narcissistic, fist-pounding materialists who lead with a "my way or the highway" style and put their needs above all else. While such an approach does account for why many people ascend to corner offices[20], you would be wrong if you assumed that Ken Olsen used that kind of tactic to succeed. You would also be very wrong to assume that the aspects of a narcissistic personality that interfere with effective management—extreme grandiosity and a sense of entitlement—were the cause of his undoing.

No, hubris was not the cause of Ken Olsen's undoing. The FORTUNE article[1] and those close to Olsen indicate that he was more humble than arrogant.[*] A truly religious man,

---

[*] From 1976 to 1999 I was affiliated with Harvard Medical School's flagship psychiatric facility, McLean Hospital. While there, several senior executives from *DEC* were psychotherapy patients of mine. They corroborated every point presented in this analysis of Ken Olsen

Olsen donated large sums of his vast wealth to a foundation that supported Christian philanthropies. Outside of work Olsen was even more wholesome. Although he was an auto buff who could afford any car he wanted, Olsen drove an Escort station wagon to work. He also hated being seen in his wife's Mercedes.

Was it Complacency?

There is a large body of research that has examined how businesses suffer paradoxical reactions to success that are maladaptive.[5] There are a variety of explanations for why success breeds failure, but where this phenomenon is most acutely obvious is in the entrepreneurial sector, the one Olsen operated in. Possible explanations for the problems entrepreneurial ventures have following the struggles of getting into the black are that they become risk-avoidant once money starts rolling in either because of complacency[22] or because they believe their business plan need not be reexamined. Consequently, they miss the opportunities that rapidly growing competitors see in changing or expanding environments.[12]

Regardless of what processes are at work when successful businesses grow complacent and fail to innovate, two things are true. First, rewards are not what they are cracked up to be and results are never good enough; Wall Street is fickle and demands growth. Second, businesses need to stay hungry, not stay happy, to remain successful. Although the lessons of corporate implosions following success are relevant to executives who fall victim to their own success, factors involving diffusion of responsibility, mistrust of others, and groupthink make organizational decline a separate phenomenon.

Perseveration, the Silent Killer

Armchair Freudians looking for the complex that drove Olsen to self-destruct will not find a psychodynamic smoking gun. Rather, Olsen acted the way he did because of his success and how success is viewed in American culture. Over the years, in both my psychotherapy practice with executives and my executive coaching work, I have concluded that successful people risk becoming victims of their own success because of the manner in which being labeled a success changes their self-conception.

Before he achieved success and became CEO of a billion-dollar corporation, I believe that Ken Olsen would have been receptive to developing personal computers and less stubborn about pushing the mini-computers he designed. Success changed how Olsen thought about the world in ways that prevented him from modifying his behavior. Success caused Olsen to repeat the behaviors that worked so brilliantly during the hey-day of his career.

I call this form of self-destructive behavior *perseveration*: an apparently conscious insistence by successful people to cling to formerly tried-and-true problem-solving strategies despite their present ineffectiveness.[10] Perseveration may look like a simple instance of conditioned behavior—that which has been reinforced will be repeated—but it is not. First, in classical conditioning, intermittent reinforcement (rewarding responses randomly or at staggered intervals) creates the strongest habits. Successful people do not receive intermittent reinforcement but, instead, are continuously reinforced.[2] Second, habit patterns that develop through classical conditioning are readily extinguished with punishment or the removal of rewards. The aspect of perseveration that marks it as self-destructive is that it takes on a life of its own as the motivation to engage in it grows despite a lack of reinforcement.

The Causes of Perseveration

From analyzing executives who have self-destructed as a result of perseveration, I have determined that this pattern of behavior emerges from three causes.[10] First, Americans are awed by success and project a "halo" around the head of those who achieve it, signifying they can do no wrong, no matter what endeavor. Second, the halo projected onto successful Americans not only influences how observers view and describe them, but over time, it biases how successful people view and describe themselves. Finally, perseveration is, like all self-defeating behaviors, a strategy for self-protection.

The value of understanding the three ways that success victimizes those who achieve it by causing perseveration is that it can inform interventions to prevent this destructive behavior from becoming entrenched in an executive's repertoire.

The halo effect. I used to watch Johnny Carson's late-night talk show when I was working as a postdoctoral fellow at Harvard Medical School. I was there on a Career Scientist Award from the National Institute of Mental Health for my research on self-handicapping alcohol abuse and paid close attention to information on all forms of substance abuse. The picture was grim; in virtually every demographic group surveyed, abuse was on the rise.

One evening I watched as Johnny interviewed a quarterback whose team had won the Super Bowl. One part of the exchange grabbed my attention. I recall it going something like this:

> *Johnny:* You're a hero to tens of thousands of kids. It's a terrible thing that drug abuse is killing so many of them. What would you do about this epidemic?

> *Quarterback:* Johnny, I really think that role models can help stop this problem. I'm going to do as many commercials as I can to tell kids to not use drugs. *[Wild applause from the studio audience followed.]*

I was astounded by what I heard. All I could think of was that hundreds of millions of dollars were being spent by the federal government to address drug abuse with little to no effect. Then I wondered what made a brilliant comedian think that a superbly talented athlete could crack an epidemiological nut that thousands of M.D.'s, Ph.D.'s, and law-enforcement officials found as impregnable as Fort Knox?

The answer is what psychologists call the halo effect: the tendency for an overall positive impression to bleed over and enhance evaluations of other, more specific characteristics.[27] The halo effect explains why Johnny Carson took at face value the idea that a Super Bowl winning quarterback could also stop a substance abuse epidemic.

Implicit theories of success. The halo effect plays a central role in the downfall of successful individuals because of the halo's power to anchor and enhance *implicit theories of personality*—the systems of rules that enable us to form opinions of others based upon minimal pieces of data such as gestures, physical appearance, or bits of conversation. As anyone who has been pigeonholed by an implicit theory knows, the theory is organized in ways that are highly resistant to disconfirmation. This is because it forms when people focus selectively on certain characteristics as being central and view other characteristics as peripheral. Thus, one single piece of salient data—such as being a success—is often a sufficient hook on which to hang one's implicit personality theory of the successful individual.

On some occasions—such as when prejudicial judgments arise—implicit theories are derived from personal histories. Typically, however, they are conditioned by our culture. Not surprisingly, the major cultural determinant of implicit personality theories turns out to be our language. This is why an implicit personality theory based on an attribute rich in connotations (e.g. success), will be both expansive (i.e. it is generalized to many areas) and highly resistive to disconfirmation. Moreover, owing to how our language naturally pairs certain adjectives, it is actually hard to speak in terms that violate our implicit theories. Doubt it? Try getting a mental picture of my colleague, an "extremely successful 'Mamma's boy'" (see more on this topic in Jones & Gerard[15]).

A classic series of social psychology studies demonstrated how single attributes could overwhelm and dominate the formation of implicit theories.[4,17] The aim of the experiments was to see how manipulating the adjectives *warm* versus *cold* in a brief description would affect judgments of a person. In one experiment, student volunteers were asked to rate a (fake) guest lecturer. Before the lecture, students were informed that he was either "a rather *warm* person, industrious, critical, practical, and determined," or "a rather *cold* person, industrious, critical, practical, and determined." The results of this manipulation were startling: After giving a 20-minute talk, the lecturer—who was played by the same person in each condition—left the classroom and students were asked to rate their impressions of him. Observers who monitored the faux lecture noted that students who were told the lecturer was *warm* initiated far more interactions with him than those who were told he was *cold*. As predicted, the *warm* lecturer was seen as generous, good-natured, happy, humorous, and humane, while the *cold* lecturer was judged to be ungenerous, unhappy, irritable, humorless, and ruthless.

Manipulating the adjectives *warm* versus *cold* had a major impact on how a person was judged. Can you imagine how consequential manipulating *successful* versus *failed* would have been? If not, ask yourself why successful performers, athletes, and executives—with no expertise in governance or social policy—are so readily elected to public office, while Ph.D.'s in government or urban studies struggle to convince voters that they are fit to govern?

One reason successful stars make popular political candidates and merely intelligent and educated people do not, is that successful people generate far more appealing associations in our implicit personality theories. Evidence of this can be found in maxims regarding how successful people function. We know that anyone who is a success is indefatigable, particularly under pressure, since "when the going gets tough, the tough get going." Similarly, those who achieve success, "never say die," are more than able to "stand the heat," and won't "pass the buck" since they believe, just as President Truman's famous desk sign declared, "The buck stops here!" Finally, should a successful person *not* succeed at first, rest easy: he or she will "try, try again."

Ken Olsen's Halo. The FORTUNE article that called Ken Olsen America's most successful entrepreneur claimed that he changed the way people use computers. While changing how we use computers, he received an incalculable number of accolades and internalized the vast majority of them. Thus, owing to our implicit personality theories about successful people, how could Olsen have concluded anything other than, "Good Lord, I'm great! I should push the mini-computer; it revolutionized the world. Why pay attention to those kids in Silicon Valley and their PC toys?"

Stated another way, Olsen became a victim of success as a result of the first two causes of perseveration; he had a halo projected onto him because of the stellar success he led at DEC, and as a result, it changed his thinking: he came to believe in the halo himself.

While I have never spoken with Olsen, I have had many conversations with individuals suffering from perseveration. Based on those interactions, I imagine success virtually brainwashed Olsen to behave as he did because he thought something like, "I know that the mini-computer will prevail over time. I've been correct before; I'll be correct again."

A Rose by any Other Name

Ram Charan and Geoffrey Colvin's June 21, 1999 cover story in FORTUNE magazine didn't claim that what causes most CEOs to fail was perseveration, but it should have. What these authors set out to do in that article was answer the question, "How do CEOs blow it?" They concluded, "The failure [of CEOs] is one of emotional strength."[11] Later, Charan and Colvin noted that a major cause of many a CEO's undoing was failing to remove subordinates who performed poorly in a timely manner.

Charan and Colvin misspoke slightly. On the surface it appeared as though the CEOs' problems boiled down to failing to fire subordinates when appropriate. What was truly at issue was the fact that the CEOs stuck with their own bad staffing decisions far too long, in the face of evidence that the decisions were poor ones, and despite feedback that their decisions were leading to failed outcomes. That, in a nutshell, is perseveration.

Charan and Colvin did, however, get it right when they stated, "most failed CEOs were psychologically incapable of reversing decisions they made" to put a person in a key position "despite recognizing that it was wrong." "What is striking," they noted, "is that [CEOs] usually know there's a problem; their inner voice is telling them, but they suppress it." As one CEO said, "It was staring me in the face but I refused to see it."

Old dogs, new tricks.

The third cause of perseveration is the self-protective nature of this ostensibly self-defeating behavior pattern. Outward appearances not withstanding, all self-defeating behaviors are governed by what Freud called the *pleasure principle*. That is, they bring some measure of gratification. The unique aspect of self-defeating behaviors is that they also cause collateral damage that outweighs the immediate rewards.

A classic example of self-defeating behavior is substance abuse, from cocaine to chocolate. Concerning chocolate, well-intended friends may say, "A moment on the lips, a lifetime on the hips," to underscore that while chocolate can be a tasty stress-reducer or psychic reward, it is a self-destructive habit when consumed in excess. They argue, "Why not stop after one bite— or before taking bite one—and seek an alternative reward?" Stated another way, "If you know you will regret it down the road, why not get off the highway?"

When considering self-defeating disorders such as the addictions and codependency, it is obvious that what keeps a person locked in patterns of defeat is a matrix of psychological, physiological, biochemical, and social factors. Not so with perseveration. With this self-defeating behavior, the puzzling question is, "Why do super-smart and capable people fail to use their abilities to continually adapt and instead resist new information when it is obvious that the old way is working against them?"

Professor Chris Argyris has examined this issue thoroughly.[2,3] Dr. Argyris' research reveals why "smart, old dogs" are adamantly opposed to learning new tricks. As he explains it, the motive is simple: Resistance to dropping old solutions and learning new strategies stems from a universal human tendency to have our behavior satisfy four basic needs:[2] to feel like we are in control, to maximize winning and minimize losing, to suppress negative feelings, and to appear to behave rationally in accordance with clear and rational objectives.

The purpose of behaving in accordance with these values is consistent with the view espoused by virtually all humanistic and "positive" psychologists—to avoid embarrassment or threat to one's favorable self-image. Thus, those old dogs are loath to try new tricks for fear of looking stupid or inept. And don't try pushing them with words of encouragement such as, "Come on, Fido; given all the tricks you know, this one will be easy." As Argyris points out, the simple act of encouraging, let alone demanding, that an individual examine or abandon behavioral repertoires that have been successful, will almost certainly be seen as an intimidation tactic and arouse greater resistance to learning and change.

Argyris brings a wealth of insight to this issue. He makes one point, however, about why successful people are prone to resisting efforts to teach them that is crucial to understanding perseveration: It is the paradox of being victimized by a history of success. According to Argyris, a successful person's

> ...very success at education helps explain the problems they have with
> learning. Before they enter the world of work, their lives are primarily full
> of successes so they have rarely experienced the embarrassment and sense

of threat that comes with failure. As a result, their defensive reasoning has rarely been activated. *People who rarely experience failure, however, end up not knowing how to deal with it effectively*. And this serves to reinforce the normal human tendency to reason defensively. [2]

Any clinician who has treated phobic patients will tell you that once you get a phobic who has never envisioned a worst-case scenario to do so, it is not uncommon to have long-standing avoidant behaviors melt away. But as long as boogeymen are allowed to lurk undisturbed in the shadows, their powers to intimidate grow stronger and stronger.

Sewell Avery and Montgomery Ward & Co.

Sewell Avery, former CEO and Chairman of Montgomery Ward & Co., had a massive resistance to learning. While his company was in a position of dominance in the retail industry during his early years at the helm, Avery blocked all attempts to expand Montgomery Ward's business to the suburbs from 1941 to 1957. In fact, Avery did not open a single new store during that period, a business strategy that ultimately led to the bankruptcy of Montgomery Ward.[28]

Avery thought he was a brilliant businessman who needed no help; his imperious attitude reflected that self-assessment. The problem—common to people who become victims of their own success—was that Avery's attitude was acquired the old-fashioned way... he earned it.

Born into a prosperous family, Avery obtained a law degree and went to work at a company that soon merged with several others to form the United States Gypsum Company. When the dust settled, Avery was president of the new conglomerate. By running an extraordinarily tight ship at Big Gyp (as the conglomerate was called), Avery proved to be the right man for the job. He turned the enterprise from a regional company into a dominant national building materials concern. While Avery was able to grow Big Gyp during the boom time of the roaring 1920s, he did not take the success for granted. Having come of age in the depressed 1890s, Avery had learned to see every glass as half empty. In fact, he so distrusted the future that he was known in the business world as Gloomy Sewell.

Avery didn't look so gloomy by the end of the 1920s; circumstances made him appear positively clairvoyant. Because Avery squirreled away $35 million in retained earnings and Big Gyp had almost no long-term debt, his company not only survived the Great Depression, it thrived. Meanwhile, things weren't so rosy at Montgomery Ward. Its management had been perennially overoptimistic and had taken a bath in the short, sharp depression of 1920–1921. One of Montgomery Ward's principal stockholders, J. P. Morgan himself, personally persuaded Avery to take over Montgomery Ward and clean house. It was an offer Sewell could not refuse.

In the first three years of the Avery regime, 22,000 out of a total of 35,000 employees left Montgomery Ward. After achieving stability, Avery guided the company to become the world's top retailer. It retained that position during the post-World War II boom years until

Avery ceased developing and expanding the chain, despite objections from his subordinates who advocated joining in the nation's postwar expansion to the suburbs.

But the brilliant "old dog" Avery would have none of that "new trick" approach. Instead of considering it, he relied upon the tried-and-true approach that worked at Big Gyp, and hoarded piles of cash. When asked to defend his strategy, he scoffed that history was on his side. He showed anyone who questioned his judgment a chart he had prepared demonstrating that a depression followed every major war since those waged by Napoleon. "Who am I to argue with history?" Avery taunted those with the temerity to disagree with him. "Why build $14-a-foot buildings [in the suburbs now] when we can soon do it for $3-a-foot?"

Had a depression come, Avery would have looked like a genius; but it did not. As a result of Avery's intransigence, Montgomery Ward & Co. never caught up with chains like Sears that moved to the suburbs, and it was forced to close its doors forever in July of 1997.

Many organizational psychologists have examined the phenomenon of leaders self-destructing by pursuing business policies that look to be throwing good money after bad or using sunk costs to justify the continuation of a flawed plan. Studies of so-called "escalation of commitment" contend that executives cannot extricate themselves from losing courses of action because they feel responsible for sunk costs and suffer cognitive distortions that, for example, permit them to maintain their illusion of control.[24,25,26]

While it is hard to dispute this theorizing, it is cumbersome when contrasted with the elegance of Argyris' reasoning. By avoiding exposure to anything that may force them to admit a mistake or imperfection, people who have a history devoid of failure refuse to modify their behavioral strategies through two mechanisms: one, ignoring or suppressing contradictory information, and, two, psychologically distorting feedback that casts their judgment in a critical light. As Argyris notes, "most people [behave in a] profoundly defensive [manner]. Defensive reasoning encourages individuals to keep private the premises, inferences, and conclusions that shape their behavior and to avoid testing them in a truly independent, objective fashion."[2] In other words, you become a victim of your success when success makes you too smart to learn you are about to fail.

Can Victims Of Their Own Success Be Helped?

Dealing with individuals about to fall victim to their own success is no picnic. They are saddled by two major problems that preventative interventions must address—or they will be blocked from changing by their attitude that they are too smart to learn. The first problem is that victims of their own success bring the hang-ups that hamper their career to any and all remedial relationships they enter. In other words, it is not sufficient to simply say, for example, "Hey, smart old dog, I know you're made anxious when asked to learn new tricks on the job, but heck, this situation is different, so rest easy."

The second problem has to do with self-perception. Although victims of their own success are not disturbed in ways that meet clinical criteria for a psychological disorder, their self-concepts have been corrupted. Despite indisputable evidence of achievement, these individuals live with a self-image that needs ongoing reinforcement.[16]

Problem One: Resisting Help

There are many executives who mount resistance to learning because attempting to do so may prove to be embarrassing. As Argyris describes it, the problem is widespread, affecting all levels of an organizational hierarchy. Should a manager be referred to coaching for a too-smart-to-learn syndrome, the defensive posture that he will bring to the process will demand a Herculean effort from the coach. Many coaches lapse into making psychodynamic evaluations or they attempt to deal with resistance directly. I not only warn against these practices because they will prove to be ineffective—unless the coach is a skilled psychotherapist—but also because engaging in them without proper training is potentially dangerous and unethical.[9]

How, then, can a smart old dog be helped by a coach to (a) recognize resistance to learning new tricks; (b) muster the courage to risk embarrassment in attempting to learn new tricks; and (c) approach the learning process in a healthy manner, not a competitive one, that makes true mastery secondary to impressing the coach? While every coach has preferred methods for addressing these concerns, I approach these cases by first removing resistances, and then by providing a safe context that enables executives to risk not knowing, in order to learn.

Remove resistance. I find it helpful to break down resistance to treatment with the therapeutic technique called *paradoxical intervention.*[23] This intervention works with successful people because it engages their intellect and provokes them, without their knowing it, to help themselves. Paradoxical interventions are neither complex, nor steeped in arcane theory; they are easy to use as an adjunct to traditional coaching techniques.

The value of using paradoxical interventions to break the resistance of successful old dogs is that they circumvent the need to engage in convoluted attempts to interpret the emotional underpinnings of an individual's aversion to learning and behavior change. Paradoxical interventions break resistances by pulling the executive in the direction of the resistance, and never giving any attention to why the resistance exists.

To use the lingua franca of the medical profession, when you employ a paradoxical intervention, the symptom is prescribed, or at minimum, the patient is encouraged *to not change* his behavior. I have even gone so far as to actually encourage clients to increase symptoms, all for one purpose: to expose clients to the absurdity of their resistance so they will recognize its adverse consequences. When they ultimately do, it is assumed clients will either abandon their resistances or seek remediation for their symptoms. Consider the following hypothetical exchange between Sewell Avery and a coach using paradoxical intervention:

> *Coach:* I understand that there is strife with your executive team; how can I help you?
> *Sewell Avery:* Well, they refuse to understand the lessons of history... I would like them to be more open and understanding of the lessons I have drawn from history.

Coach: And what lessons would those be?

Sewell Avery: That a depression followed every major war since those waged by Napoleon. Since we just ended a war, another economic depression is around the corner.

Coach: Sounds like unassailable logic to me. Are you making preparations for that inevitability?

Sewell Avery: You bet I am! I'm doing exactly what I did before the Great Depression: hoarding cash. It saved me and Big Gyp, and it will save Montgomery Ward too, but these kids refuse to learn the lessons I did.

Coach: Are you doing anything else?

Sewell Avery: No, why do you ask?

Coach: Oh, I don't know... What if this depression is greater than the Great One?

Sewell Avery: What makes you think it will be?

Coach: I don't know; isn't more at stake?

Sewell Avery: I guess that as a nation we have more wealth, but so what?

Coach: Maybe you should start initiating layoffs as well as amassing cash.

Sewell Avery: I care about our employees and value them deeply. If I'm correct and we weather the recession, I want to keep good people around so we will have the staff to take advantage of rock-bottom prices in the real estate market. But, I'm not adverse to using pink slips when needed... I had thousands printed when I turned around Big Gyp.

Coach: But you're not holding on to real estate today, why hold on to human capital? Why not cut everything to the bone and hunker down? Why not add Big Gyp-like layoffs to your current savings plan and be doubly prepared for that recession?

Sewell Avery: Isn't that a little Draconian? Besides, training good people is costly. Are you implying that I'm saving too much money? Because if you are, I have charts...

Coach: No, you just said you're saving too much; I said you could cut more!

This session of a paradoxical intervention is only one of a series that would be needed to get a client like Mr. Avery to push back against a coach and, ultimately, realize that his perseveration and resistances were maladaptive. The point at which the coach would zero in is when the executive coach and Avery discussed layoffs. After several paradoxical interventions regarding that issue, it would not be surprising for Avery to come to the realization that his intransigence about expansion may actually result in laying off the very workers he is loath to fire.

A safe learning opportunity. Most executive coaches do not deal with clients who resist help. Executives who once feared coaching because it was confused with therapy now see it as a badge of honor. For this reason, coaches may not know that the moment they break through a client's resistance they must have a next step ready and waiting. The next step is something to engage the executive and, literally, distract him from the fact that he has made himself vulnerable to evaluation. This is crucial because the vulnerability an executive experiences will be novel, and potentially overwhelming, if not handled appropriately.

The smart old dog who is ready to learn new tricks can benefit immediately from bibliotherapy: learning via reading or studying case material that describes how other comparably successful old dogs, also leaders of the pack, not only did not die of humiliation when they left their comfort zones, but went on to thrive.

Following bibliotherapy, I recommend that coaches engage their executive clients in a protracted course of role-playing. This intervention includes two phases. The first phase consists of having the executive assume the role of mentor or coach to a colleague, played by the coach, who is grappling with his or her own too-smart-to-learn dilemma. During this exercise, the coach mirrors adaptive responses. Prior to switching from bibliotherapy to role-playing, coaches must not forget the benefit of putting successful executives in a superior role during the coaching process. When it comes to successful old dogs that are too smart to learn, this is often imperative in order to quell their competitive strivings.

The coach needs to modify the role-play for phase two. During a coaching session similarly simulated for the first phase, interrupt the executive (while in role) and pose a problem for him to solve that he did not anticipate. By doing so, the executive will experience anxiety in a safe environment, and with the coach's supervision, be forced to cope with the unforeseen problem. Negative feedback to the client is crucial at this point. If a coach can be critical yet supportive, the old dog can generalize the learning principle and approach any context demanding he learn new tricks with equanimity.

Problem Two: Self-conception

Narcissistic instabilities have traditionally been linked to patterns of parenting that make people feel objectified.[6] Or, in a description I prefer, people believe they have been loved for what they produce, not loved for who they *are*. Paradoxically, both parental overindulgence and emotional neglect have been noted as causes of an unstable sense of self in adults, as has unpredictable and inconsistent care-giving.[13]

Most often, however, studies of what causes narcissistic instability in children conclude that the culprit is parenting marked by excessive admiration but not balanced with realistic feedback.[18] Specifically, the scenario most damaging to a developing child's sense of self is receiving laudatory feedback and not knowing why, save for the fact that, "Mom and dad say so." As a result of this developmental scenario, a child is driven to wonder, "Maybe they're telling me this stuff to get me to strive for even greater heights?" As a consequence, the child constantly struggles to gain certainty of his worth lest he be forced to conclude that his fear, "They really *don't love me* for just *me*," is accurate.[21]

Being confused in this manner by excessive positive feedback can establish a vulnerability in those who are on the path to becoming a victim of their own success. As adults, they are likely to have difficulty enjoying their success and will neither be able to dissociate themselves from their personal success nor foster the success of others.[8]
The significance of not being able to either enjoy success or dissociate oneself from it and nurture the development of others has a profound influence on a coach's ability to plan interventions for a victim of his own success. First, when a person is focused on meeting internalized expectations for success not yet attained, his experience of his achievements is incomplete. The metaphor I use is that these people feel like ancient and incredibly valuable Ming vases with holes in the bottom. They believe they are extraordinarily valuable, albeit damaged, because they cannot be filled with fluid. (Even though one would not necessarily fill a Ming vase, hang on for a moment—the metaphor works.)

Feeling damaged, these individuals constantly seek to redress the damage. If a halo is projected on them, they wear it, not questioning why, since it may help in damage control. On the other hand, if novel learning opportunities are presented to them (not as a repair kit, but posing the potential for embarrassment), they reject it. Moreover, the "damaged" Ming vase never thinks, "Lord Almighty! I'm worth millions just standing empty or holding dried twigs despite this little hole in my base." It's a classic case of focusing on the hole, not the donut.

Redirect the need to achieve. As long as an executive locked in a pattern of perseveration focuses on the hole and needs to strive for more and greater successes, there is no saving him from becoming a victim of his own success. The primary goal of coaching must be to find some intervention to help him find value and reward apart from accomplishment—of status and tangible manifestations of self-esteem—for change to occur.

While this is no mean feat, it is not impossible. What I like to do at the outset of relationships with executives who perseverate is exploit the fact that virtually all of them have either been entrepreneurs (like Ken Olsen) or originators of the business model that they stubbornly refuse to abandon. As such, they have an entrepreneurial spirit buried somewhere inside that can be tapped into and drawn out for their own good. The key is, once this spirit is identified, it cannot be left alone to operate on its own. A coach's guidance is needed.

To guide the spirit, a coach must find an issue, cause, or activity that provokes a perseverating executive's interest. In Ken Olsen's case, I would have focused on Catholic charities, something about which he was passionate. The next crucial step in the coaching process is to provoke the executive to get angry, in a constructive manner, with regard to the issue he is passionate about. Now the coach can begin the process of disengaging perseveration.

The problem with the manner in which most successful people support causes they feel passionate about is that they do it with checkbooks rather than voting with their feet. While at DEC, Olsen wrote checks to various Catholic charities and once every so often attended a prayer breakfast. Good for him, but not good for tens of thousands of Catholics who would have benefited for example, if he had developed a program to start Computers for Catholics. Had Olsen's hypothetical coach induced him to embark upon this sort of program, the wisdom behind the idea would have been irresistible: "Of course," Olsen would agree, "I want to help give the impoverished members of my Archdiocese access to the computing resources they cannot possibly have unless they work in corporations that own DEC mini-computers!" Then, proceeding over time, through either guided dialogue, a business plan development, or simulated board meetings, Olsen's coach would urge him—as a good Catholic and great engineer—to throw himself into the project.

In my experience, adding an entrepreneurial venture of this sort to the life of a CEO engaged in perseveration is not only stimulating, it is an antidote to burnout.[8] Entrepreneurial activity is both challenging and reinforcing, not to mention capable of eliciting endorphins that produce biochemical reactions resembling a runner's high. If Ken Olsen got engaged in doing the Lord's work in his engineering space, the DEC colleagues who were lobbying for desktop computers—those "toys from Silicon Valley"—might continue to drop into his office and bug him. As Louis Pasteur said: "Chance favors the prepared mind."

Back to our hypothetical coaching session:

> *Olsen:* How can I help the kids in the Archdiocese?
> *Colleagues:* Ken, what about the PC?
> *Coach:* Ken, any progress with your attempts to launch 'Computers for Catholics'?
> *Olsen:* Mercy Sakes! Maybe, since we're talking about kids in the Archdiocese whose computing needs are not sophisticated, not business executives who need state-of-the-art applications, maybe I can give that 'toy' from Silicon Valley a try? When you think about it, it could be a perfect match!

Detachment

When I examined the causes of burnout in successful executives, I found that not being able to detach oneself from societal demands for ever-increasing levels of achievement was a major cause.[8] When an executive with a metaphorical hole in his Ming vase cannot extricate himself from acting in ways intended to dominate market sectors, control industries, or conquer new heights, this action orientation becomes a hindrance.[19] If an executive you know is obsessed with success at all costs and cannot experience himself as a Ming vase simply holding twigs, irrespective of "that hole," and has no time for the process of caring for the next generation or nurturing others—what the famed psychoanalyst Erik Erikson[14] called generativity—he needs help.

The problem is this: developing the self-reflective capacity needed to both cede control of the process of striving for success and foster the development of others is not something one derives from traditional coaching interventions. It can be a consequence of long-term therapy, but most executives eschew this process while in the midst of becoming a victim of their own success. For these reasons, what I recommend for the individuals I coach who need boosts in their self-reflective strength is a *Rabbi*, irrespective of what religious affiliation (if any) they have. Here I am using the term *Rabbi* as it is used on Wall Street, to mean a trusted advisor.

A good Rabbi is ideally older than an executive, very familiar with the people and the field in which the executive works, and, most of all, at peace with himself. A Rabbi's work can supplement coaching; a good Rabbi will not interfere with anyone helping an old dog learn new tricks. What he will do is help an executive stop and smell the roses long enough to recognize that the maniacal pursuit of success is counterproductive.

And so we return to Twain: "Faith is believing what you know ain't so." Rabbis force you to question your faith and allow you to *not* believe what you know ain't so. When you question your faith in pursuing success at all costs, you can enjoy what you have achieved, know it is real, ask, "Was it worth it?" and move on. It is the ability to move on with equanimity that inoculates executives against becoming victims of their own success.

References

1. America's most successful entrepreneur. (1986, October 27). *Fortune*, 24-32.

2. Argyris, C. (1991). Teaching smart people how to learn. *Harvard Business Review, 69*(3), 99-109.

3. Argyris, C. (1994). Good communication that blocks learning. *Harvard Business Review, 72*(4), 77-85.

4. Asch, S. E. (1946). Forming impressions of personality. *Journal of Abnormal and Social Psychology, 41*, 258-290.

5. Audia, P. G., Locke, E. A., & Smith, K. G. (2000). The paradox of success: An archival and a laboratory study of strategic persistence following radical environmental change. *The Academy of Management Journal, 43*, 837-853.

6. Baker, H. S., & Baker, M. N. (1987). Heinz Kohut's psychology of the self: An overview. *American Journal of Psychiatry, 144*, 1-9.

7. Berglas, S. (1986). *The success syndrome: Hitting bottom when you reach the top.* New York: Plenum.

8. Berglas, S. (2001). *Reclaiming the fire: How successful people overcome burnout.* New York: Random House.

9. Berglas, S. (2002). The very real dangers of executive coaching. *Harvard Business Review, 80*(6), 86-92.

10. Berglas, S., & Baumeister, R. F. (1993). *Your own worst enemy: Understanding the paradox of self-defeating behavior.* New York: Basic Books.

11. Charan, R., & Colvin, G. (1999, June 21). Why CEO's fail. *Fortune*, 69-82.

12. Churchill, N. C., & Lewis, V. L. (1983). The five stages of small business growth. *Harvard Business Review, 61*(3), 30-50.

13. Cooper A. M. (1984). Narcissism in normal development. In M. Zales (Ed.), *Character pathology* (pp. 39-56). New York: Brunner/Mazel.

14. Erikson, E. H. (1968). *Identity, youth, and crisis.* New York: Norton.

15. Jones, E. E., & Gerard, H. B. (1967). *Foundations of social psychology.* New York: Wiley.

16. Kaplan, R. E., & Kaiser, R. B. (in press). Towards a positive psychology for leaders. In P. A. Linley, S. Harrington, & N. Page (Eds.), *Oxford Handbook of Positive Psychology and Work.* New York: Oxford University Press.

17. Kelly, H. H. (1950). The warm-cold variable in first impressions of persons. *Journal of Personality, 18*, 431-439.

18. Kernberg, O. F. (1984). *Severe personality disorders: Psychotherapeutic strategies.* New Haven, CT: Yale University Press.

19. Kramer, R. M. (2003). The harder they fall. *Harvard Business Review, 81*(5), 58-66.

20. Maccoby, M. (2000). Narcissistic leaders: The incredible pros, the inevitable cons. *Harvard Business Review, 78*(1), 68-78.

21. Miller, A. (1981). *Prisoners of childhood*. New York: Basic Books.

22. Miller, J., & Chen, M. J. (1994). Sources and consequences of competitive inertia. *Administrative Science Quarterly*, *39*, 1-23.

23. Seltzer, L. F. (1986). *Paradoxical strategies in psychotherapy: A comprehensive overview and guidebook*. New York: Wiley.

24. Staw, B. M. (1981). The escalation of commitment to a course of action. *Academy of Management Review, 6*, 577–587.

25. Staw, B. M. (1997). The escalation of commitment: An update and appraisal. In Z. Shapira (Ed.), *Organization decision making* (pp. 191–215). New York: Cambridge University Press.

26 Staw, B. M., & Ross, J. (1987). Knowing when to pull the plug. *Harvard Business Review, 65*(2), 68-74.

27. Thorndike, E. L. (1920). A constant error in psychological ratings. *Journal of Applied Psychology, 4*, 469-477.

28. You snooze, you lose. (1997, July 21). *Newsweek*, 50.

SECTION 3

Weaknesses Matter

CHAPTER 7

MANAGERIAL DERAILMENT
Weaknesses that can be Fixed

William A. Gentry & Craig T. Chappelow
Center for Creative Leadership

Most of us have seen it happen. And, just as with a real train wreck, we know we shouldn't gawk when we see managerial derailment occur, but it can seem so disastrous and compelling at the same time that we can't help ourselves. This may be for good reason: there is much to learn from studying managerial derailment and its close connection to weaknesses.

Originally, the term derailment was reserved for talented managers who shot up the fast track and reached a senior leadership position but ultimately did not go as far as expected. But derailment is not just an executive phenomenon; it also takes a toll on middle-level managers.[15,40] Regardless of the level at which they flame out, derailment is defined as having one's advancement stall despite a desire to continue rising or, even worse, getting demoted or fired. Though the Center for Creative Leadership (CCL) began studying derailment over 25 years ago with McCall and Lombardo's[33] seminal report, *Off the Track*, the risk of managerial derailment is just as relevant today—perhaps even more than managers think.

In 1944 Bing Crosby and the Andrews Sisters encouraged us to "accentuate the positive." But we tend to forget the next line, "eliminate the negative." Maybe they were warning us about the danger of focusing exclusively on our strengths—that accentuating the positives can blind us to our weaknesses. And if that happens, managers are bound for peril, particularly if the weaknesses they ignore are those characteristic of derailed managers.

This chapter focuses on the causes of managerial derailment and the important patterns of weaknesses that go along with it. We first discuss the surprisingly high failure rate of managers and reasons for their ineffectiveness. We then discuss the history of managerial derailment research and describe the five fatal flaws that lead to derailment: (1) Problems with Interpersonal Relationships, (2) Difficulty Leading a Team, (3) Difficulty Changing or Adapting, (4) Failure to Meet Business Objectives, and (5) Too Narrow of a Functional Orientation. We use real-world examples of managers to illustrate these flaws. Finally, we close the chapter with practical suggestions for managers and organizations to avoid derailment.

Managerial (In)effectiveness

From the pointy-haired boss in Dilbert cartoons to the dysfunctional manager in the TV series, "The Office," images and stories of the bumbling and inept manager have become the stuff of popular media. More problematically, it is discussed behind the backs of those real-world managers in company cafeterias and office cubicles. Two questions may come to mind. First, are derailing managers really such a prevalent part of organizational life—or does it just make for good TV? Should organizations even be concerned? And second, if derailment really is a problem, what can be done to address it?

Derailment is expensive. C-level executives may have buyout clauses in their contracts. Even replacing lower-level managers is expensive, time consuming, and disruptive. If the organization has to make a new hire, time and money is spent on recruitment, selection, and on-boarding. Millions or billions of dollars could be lost annually due to ineffective managers.[12,42,48] Money aside, executive derailment can be devastating to the individual, can have negative impact on customers, and can adversely affect the morale of coworkers, especially those who worked closely with the failed manager.[13,16]

Managerial ineffectiveness is more common than many people think. Table 1 shows the estimated failure rates of managers in different research studies over recent decades. Surprisingly these data show that one out of every two managers is expected to eventually fail.

Table 1.
Estimated Failure Rates for Managers From Research and Experts

Study	Estimated managerial failure rate
Bentz (1985)	50%
Hogan, Curphy, & Hogan (1994)	55%
Hogan & Hogan (2001)	67%
Hogan & Kaiser (2005)	50%
Lombardo & Eichinger (1989/2005)	50%
Millikin-Davies (1992)	50%
Rogers & Smith (2004)	50%
Sessa, Kaiser, Taylor & Campbell (1998)	30%
Shipper & Wilson (1992)	60%
Sorcher (1985)	33%
White & DeVries (1990)	50%
Mean	50.5%
Median	50%

The organizational landscape is constantly changing, especially in recent times. As Eichinger, Dai, and Tang (this volume) pointed out in chapter 2, the business environment is becoming more fast-paced, competitive, dynamic, and global. At the same time, organizations spent the last 15 years downsizing and outsourcing and eventually became flat.[1,34] Add to this mix the fact that managerial work is complex and ambiguous,[25] which promotes confusion about expectations and uncertainty about how the roles of other managers "fit" in the organization.[17] These factors add up to make it incredibly difficult for managers to be effective. In many cases the odds for success are stacked against managers from the time they enter the organization.

When managers derail, younger, high-potential individuals are often required to step up and take their place. This can problematic because the talent pool is shrinking.[38] Those who are left are extremely valued by organizations, but many of these promising up-and-comers eventually fail because transitions and promotions are too quick, and they are rushed into authority before they are ready for these high-profile positions.[6,30]

In summary, organizational factors, the nature of managerial work in general, and the reduction of the talent pool may contribute to managerial ineffectiveness and failure. Yet many times, managers successfully navigate these initial obstacles and still derail. One cause might be that they have a personality flaw disposing them to failure.[2]

Hogan and Hogan[20] popularized the study of "dark side" personalities that lead managers to failure. Their research indicates that certain dark side dispositions such as arrogance, aloofness, and perfectionism are associated with managerial failure. This research has sparked interest in the relationship between specific personality variables and ineffectiveness. For instance, ineffective managers may be narcissistic[23,32] or have other dysfunctional personality styles such as being overly "suspicious" or "pessimistic" or "eccentric."[37] Some may argue that it does little good to study the dark side personalities associated with derailment because they assume that personality is set for adults,[7,8,22] which leads to the conclusion that it may be very difficult for managers to moderate ineffective behaviors. In other words, if a manager has a particular type of counter-productive personality, many would believe that the manager is destined to fail.

However, CCL's experience has shown that personality is not destiny (for a similar argument, see chapter 9 by Malcolm Davies, this volume). Those of us who propose development as a way to improve managerial effectiveness contend that development starts with coming to terms with one's own strengths and weaknesses (see chapter 8 by Hogan & Benson),[18] Once this level of self-awareness is in place, managers can take steps to change specific behaviors to neutralize or eliminate weaknesses and prevent derailment. CCL's research on managerial derailment deals entirely with behaviors, both positive and negative. If managers do not address the behavior patterns associated with these weaknesses, they increase the odds that they, too, will derail.

The good news is that derailment is preventable,[30] and executives who develop a high level of self awareness and become familiar with the warning signs of derailment as outlined in the subsequent section can create a plan for behavioral change to avoid the crisis. We will make the case that focusing exclusively on one's strengths and ignoring one's weaknesses is a recipe for disaster.

The History of Managerial Derailment Research

The earliest research comparing successful managers who progressed far in their careers to those who never rose through the ranks was conducted at AT&T.[4,5] The AT&T studies found that the managers who did not rise lacked the leadership, administrative, and career skills that successful managers had in spades. However, this research did not focus on failure per se. Research focused explicitly on managerial failure started in the 1970s with Jon Bentz's pioneering studies of failed executives at Sears, Roebuck, and Company.[2] These studies were particularly noteworthy in that Sears, a traditionally conservative company based in the

Midwestern United States, allowed Bentz to air its dirty laundry and go public with stories of high-level failure. Similar to the AT&T studies, Bentz documented how failed executives lacked some of the skills associated with success. However, he further observed that each of the failed executives had what he termed a "personality defect." More than a lack of "the right stuff," Bentz concluded that executive failure was largely the result of "the wrong stuff."

Kotter[26] discovered that failed executives did not act in a way that reinforces the importance of agenda setting and networking. Kotter also noted that failed executives were a poor fit to the demands of their jobs. Later, Gabarro[14] found that executives who failed did not have the requisite background to be successful in upper-tier executive positions, and oftentimes had a history of troubled relationships with peers, subordinates, and supervisors—a finding that raises the specter of Bentz's[2] so-called personality defects.

Behavioral Differences

Much of the previous research focused on the lack of skills or presence of dysfunctional personality factors. But many managers who failed or derailed also *behaved* differently. The study of the behaviors of derailed managers started in the early 1980s at CCL. Morgan McCall and Michael Lombardo[33] interviewed senior executives from three Fortune 500 companies and asked them to recount a person who succeeded in rising to the top of their organization as well as a person who had all the makings to achieve equal success but did not live up to his or her potential and was either demoted, fired, plateaued (i.e., stopped advancing), or opted for early retirement. This first CCL derailment study consisted of a total of 40 cases: 20 success stories and 20 stories of derailment.

Careful analysis of the interview data helped to differentiate the successful and derailed managers. However, it should be noted that the successful executives and derailed executives were amazingly similar on the surface. The derailers did not start out as problem managers. On the contrary, like the successful managers, the derailed managers had an outstanding track record, were well-liked, knew their businesses and were technologically savvy, were loyal or "good soldiers" who accepted whatever assignments they were given, and were driven and motivated. Importantly, neither the successful nor derailed managers were described as perfect.

Differences eventually emerged between the successful and derailed managers despite their striking similarities. Some of those differences were minor, but those minor differences ultimately made a major difference. Unlike the derailed managers, successful managers were considered "jacks of all trades" and performed well in a variety of assignments. Successful managers were also more poised under pressure; they were able to handle stress and dealt with their mistakes gracefully, even demonstrating an ability to harvest key lessons from those mistakes as opposed to the derailers who tended to react defensively to mistakes. The successful managers took a "whatever it takes" attitude toward problem solving. Lastly, they were able to work well with different types of people, while derailers often had relationship problems.

To illustrate the dynamics of derailment, McCall and Lombardo[33] described four reasons why executives derailed, which are still relevant today.

Strengths eventually became weaknesses. Some of the derailed managers relied too heavily on the strengths that were useful to them at the beginnings of their careers, but became liabilities in new situations. For instance, "loyalty becomes overdependence...ambition destroys their support base."[33] The once brilliant, ambitious manager comes to be seen as abrasive, treating others poorly. Independence that was once seen as a strength is later seen as a detriment because the manager can't work through a team. The manager whose strength was great technical skills had trouble making the transition to more complex roles. Taking a strong stand and defending one's position can be seen as a strength, but when overplayed, such a manager will be perceived as inflexible and perhaps even bullying—limited in the ability to influence others and unwilling to compromise. In sum, derailed managers continued to rely on what once made them successful, but was now a hindrance in their present jobs.[27]

Weaknesses evident early in a career were ignored. Other derailed managers realized they had weaknesses which, early in their careers, they could compensate for with other assets. However, as these managers progressed, they never got around to strengthening those weaknesses—and this proved to be their Waterloo. Insensitivity is a weakness that "one can get by with" at early stages of managerial work, "but not [later] when one's subordinates and peers are powerful and probably also brilliant."[33] Derailing managers do not adjust their behavior despite changing demands in their present roles.[30]

Success went to their heads. Derailed managers became prisoners of their own success. Many times, managers on the way up are shielded from negative feedback, and are continuously told how good they are, which may lead to their losing humility and becoming cold and arrogant.[24] They begin to believe their own press clippings and eventually see themselves as incapable of making a mistake. In chapter 6, Steven Berglas[3] takes a deep look at this dynamic in explaining how managers can become victims of their own success.

Stuff happens. In some of the cases, through no fault of their own, something happened in the organization that had an adverse impact. Some derailed managers were tripped up by environmental constraints, market shifts, economic downturns, politics, downsizing, buyouts, mergers and acquisitions, and just plain bad luck.

Men, Women, and Derailment

The McCall and Lombardo[33] study laid the foundation for future derailment research. One of the limitations of their study was that the subjects were all men. In response, Morrison, White, and Van Velsor[36] replicated the earlier study with interviews about women leaders in 25 companies representing a wide range of industries. Results from their interviews showed that the group of successful women, much like the men in McCall and Lombardo's study, had a good track record of past achievement. Women, however, were different than men in that they were described as having help from more senior sponsors. The successful women were also ambitious and achievement oriented, willing to take risks in their careers, and capable of being tough, decisive, and demanding yet still effective at managing their direct reports.

Though there were some similarities between derailed male managers and derailed female managers (e.g., inability to lead others), there were also differences. The most common reasons male managers derailed included insensitivity and troubled relationships, performance problems, failure to build a team, and overdependence on a particular boss or mentor. By comparison, some of the women executives who derailed had trouble adapting to a new boss or the company's culture. Some of the women who derailed were described as having a poor or negative image (i.e., style, stature, or mannerisms that adversely affected impressions). Furthermore, derailed female executives had performance issues and were perceived as overly ambitious.

Quantitative Findings

CCL's derailment research continued with Lombardo and McCauley.[31] The previous two studies were qualitative; the reasons for success and derailment were found through analyzing the answers to in-depth interviews with the successful and derailed manager's co-workers. Lombardo and McCauley, on the other hand, used a quantitative survey measure. Using a sample of over 300 managers and executives, this survey research uncovered six derailment "themes" or categories. They are (1) Problems with Interpersonal Relationships; (2) Difficulty in Molding a Staff; (3) Difficulty in Making Strategic Transitions; (4) Lack of Follow-through; (5) Overdependence on a Mentor or Advocate and (6) Strategic Differences with Management. These six themes supplied the critical theoretical framework for CCL's 360-degree assessment tool known as Benchmarks®. This developmental assessment tool provides managers with targeted feedback on the specific behaviors associated with *both* success and derailment. By focusing on their strengths *and* development needs, managers can address potential derailers before it is too late. This research reinforced the importance of not focusing on strengths to the exclusion of weaknesses associated with derailment.

Time, Culture, and Derailment

In the 1990s, researchers at CCL concluded that because the world of work had drastically changed as a result of downsizing, reengineering, and increased globalization, a replication of past derailment research was necessary to determine if derailment was still a relevant phenomenon and if so, whether the causes were the same now as in the past. Thus, Leslie and Van Velsor[29,46] interviewed 20 senior executives from 15 *Fortune 500* companies in the United States and also extended past derailment research by interviewing 42 European executives from companies based in Belgium, France, Germany, Italy, Spain, and the United Kingdom. Both samples were asked the same questions as in previous derailment research ("Describe a manager who made it to the top of his/her organization, and one who did not reach his or her expected level"). Both managerial samples also completed quantitative surveys about derailment as well. A few key findings resulted from their research. First, though many derailment themes were consistent over time, the dynamics of derailment were different, which reflected the changes in organizations already discussed (i.e., downsizing, flattening, complexity). Secondly, derailment themes in the United States were similar and consistent when compared to derailment themes found in Europe. As Van Velsor and Leslie noted, cultural values do not derail managers but rather, it is the individual manager and the lack of perceived fit with the job, role, or organization that play an important role in derailment.

Five Common Reasons for Derailment

Over the course of this program of derailment research, from the 1983 study of Morgan and McCall, through the 1995 research of Leslie and Van Velsor, several success factors remained consistent. Successful managers were ambitious, established strong relationships, were consistently high performers, had team-building and leadership skills, were intelligent, were willing to take risks, were able to adapt, and were problem-solvers.

There were also consistent derailment themes across the different derailment studies. Problems with Interpersonal Relationships, Difficulty Leading a Team, Difficulty Changing and Adapting, and Failure to Meet Business Objectives were mentioned in the studies above. A fifth derailment theme, Too Narrow of a Functional Orientation, emerged from later studies. It should be noted that Overdependence on a Mentor or Advocate, which was prevalent in early derailment studies, "dropped out" as a derailment factor in later studies.

We next discuss each of the five recurrent reasons for derailment in detail, and give real-life examples of each reason based on managers we have encountered in our work inside organizations. The names of the individuals and their organizations have been changed or omitted for reasons of confidentiality. The major point we wish to emphasize with these stories is the clear link between weaknesses and career derailment.

Derailment Factor #1: Problems with Interpersonal Relationships

Janice worked for a U.S.-based multinational pharmaceutical company. Early in her career she delivered impressive numbers, first as a sales rep, then later as a regional sales manager. Throughout her initial track record of success, she had a reputation for bringing in positive results when others failed. She had a no-nonsense approach to her work and a clear sense of right and wrong that had served her as a dependable rudder for most of her career. When asked to describe her strengths and weaknesses, Janice listed on the strengths side "I don't suffer fools easily." She also described her work style as achievement focused. When asked how she was able to accomplish what many others could not, she would often say about her approach, "I kick butt and take names, and people respond to that."

When Janice's company merged with a larger firm, the culture of the new company placed a high emphasis on collaboration. Janice was considered for, but did not receive, a promotion to vice president of sales. When she asked for the reason, all she got was jargon-laden non-answers. Months later, one of the senior executives shared with her that while they were impressed with her sales record, none of the other vice presidents wanted to work with her because of her "abrasive" (in their words) style. As one vice president put it, "She described her style as 'Kick butt and take names' but none of us wants to have our butt kicked, and she uses that approach no matter who she is dealing with."

Derailment Factor #2: Difficulty Leading a Team

Mark was a young engineer with an aeronautical design and manufacturing company who had been identified early on as a high potential employee and was placed on the fast track.

He had impressive intellectual capacity and was known for his ability to understand and resolve complicated technical problems. One of his brightest moments came when he solved a problem that no one else, including some senior engineers, had been able to fix. This was a high-stakes and high-visibility victory for the company, and solving it gave Mark's career a substantial boost.

Over the years Mark was given progressively more responsibility. There was no question in Mark's mind that he was being groomed for a senior leadership position in this organization, and he wanted nothing more. However, a pattern was emerging. Mark's direct reports complained about a lack of structure, insufficient information sharing, and little clarity of expectations. This feedback came to Mark in bits and pieces through his peers. He had a higher-than-normal rate of turnover among his direct reports, which he attributed to the impatience of younger workers and their unwillingness to "pay their dues." Mark had always believed that effectiveness was measured by results metrics—the numbers should speak for themselves. The reality was that despite the technical successes he was having, no one seemed to want to work with him. The ultimate blow came when he was passed over to lead the team that was developing a high-visibility space exploration project. This was a wake-up call for Mark, to say the least. Mark viewed himself as smart, focused on problems, and above office politics. By comparison, his coworkers saw him as arrogant, clueless about people issues, and naïve about how decisions are made. Ultimately, Mark was never able to see himself as his coworkers saw him, and he was demoted to a lower-level position where he remained until he left the company.

Derailment Factor #3: Difficulty Changing or Adapting

David, a geologist by training, invented a technology that was used for making very precise measurements of tiny objects used in the semiconductor industry. He and an associate founded a company to manufacture and sell the technology to other companies. Over the years David carried the title of CEO but was a hands-on manager, visiting each of his customers on a regular basis. With the explosion of the computer industry in the 1980s, his company grew exponentially. David insisted on calling on customers, often to the frustration of the sales staff who perceived him as getting in the way. In the meantime, David was not providing the kind of leadership the company needed in this high-growth phase and did not attend to the organization's strategy in any way but to jump from one crisis to another. The board eventually "packaged" him out of his role. To the last day of his work, David was still calling on clients, unable to evolve beyond an entrepreneurial mindset to leading a large and mature institution.

Derailment Factor #4: Failure to Meet Business Objectives

One memorable manager we met in our work at CCL was a participant in *The Looking Glass Experience*, a public CCL training program that involves a simulation during which the class participants run a fictitious glass company for a day. The group had to elect a president from among their classmates. They selected an outgoing, genuine, and impressive guy who everyone liked even though they had only been together for one day by that time. He gave a brief off-the-cuff acceptance speech, then proceeded to describe three goals for the glass company based on the brief information given to him in his in-basket. His was one of the best analyses and explanations of the task that we had ever seen. Throughout the simulation he spent a lot of time checking in with everyone, communicating openly, and did so in a warm and personable way. It seemed like the guy practically walked off of the pages of a management how-to book. He was relaxed, charming, and made everyone feel a part of the team. A real people-person.

A year later we happened to see an article in the *Wall Street Journal* that mentioned this manager had been fired for his history of disappointing results. For all his people skills and warmth, he was ultimately not able to meet his business obligations.

Derailment Factor #5: Too Narrow of a Functional Orientation

Todd was always good with numbers and with people. He excelled in math and majored in accounting in college. He was hired by a large insurance company at its headquarters near his hometown and passed the exams and training to become an actuary. Todd developed a great depth of expertise in the company's casualty business and received a series of promotions. When Todd interviewed for a director's position, he was told he did not have enough experience with the other parts of their business, nor did he have an understanding of their marketplace or competitive landscape.

We met Todd after he left the company. While some might not call this example a derailment, Todd certainly did. He was focused on achieving the director job and was crushed when he did not receive it. When we talked to him he said that in retrospect, he had been receiving informal feedback along the way that he was being pigeonholed as a casualty actuary with narrow scope. He shared that he didn't think it was important for him to be more well-rounded at the time, but now he sees that the candidate who was eventually hired had similar experience and people skills, but also had a broader perspective due to experience in other parts of the organization.

Doomed to Failure?

This review of derailment factors may lead some to believe that if a manager is displaying any of those behaviors then he or she is bound to slip off track. But that is not necessarily the case. The behaviors associated with derailment can be changed if the manager is clear about the specific behaviors that need to change, is focused and motivated to make the changes, and is supported by the organization and/or a development professional. If the signs of derailment are detected early enough, managers can turn things around and advance in their careers. The following advice can help managers and those who work with managers, such as professionals in human resources, training, coaching, and other development specialists.

Self-awareness

If knowledge is power, then self-knowledge is a superpower. Managerial self-awareness can take many shapes and forms. For instance, managers should become aware of whether or not they fit in well with their job demands, their bosses, or the people around them. Do they have a philosophical match with their organizations regarding the direction of their businesses? Many times, managers who do not enjoy the tasks that their jobs demand of them will derail. Other times, it is those managers who do not enjoy their bosses or coworkers, or just don't seem to fit in well with the company culture, who will derail. As a result, managers should often assess whether there is a "good fit" between them, their work, their coworkers, and their organizations.

Managers must become acutely aware of work overload, major life/career transitions, or boredom, which may trigger derailment as well.[10] As such, managers need to take time to reflect upon and question how they can become better managers. One of the most effective ways we know to do this is through 360-degree feedback.

Feedback

Three hundred and sixty-degree feedback is a method of systematically collecting perceptions about a manager's performance from a wide range of coworkers. This could include peers, subordinates, the boss, and the boss's peers, along with outsiders such as customers, suppliers, or vendors. CCL's 360's are designed to specifically capture both strengths and weaknesses. The resulting feedback report is issued to the participant, ideally with an opportunity to debrief the results with a neutral coach or facilitator. The assessment data generated from 360-degree feedback has two important characteristics that make it particularly rich: it is formal and it comes from multiple perspectives.

Formal feedback is important. In the life of a busy organization, managers often find themselves feedback-starved. Two factors play into this. First, managers get caught up in day-to-day pressures and responsibilities and fail to pick up the cues from others that provide one source of ongoing feedback. While waiting for the elevator after a tough meeting, a manager gets a pat on the back from her colleague for handling a tough presentation well. The next day, someone lets her know that her reaction to a sensitive question was unnecessarily defensive. At the end of the week, one of her team members cautions her that her instructions to her assistant sounded patronizing. These small bits of data—informal feedback—float around managers all the time, largely unheeded in the rush of business concerns. Formal 360-degree feedback, on the other hand, provides something that informal feedback seldom does: a structured means of collecting and compiling data, and an opportunity to reflect on this valuable information. It may be the only time a leader consciously stops to take stock of his or her performance.

Giving and receiving feedback can be threatening activities for many people, and they may not think doing either is worth the risk. This is particularly true the higher up in the organization one moves, and senior executives often receive the least feedback of anyone.[24] In modern organizations, much lip service is paid to the need to increase communication in all directions; at the same time, many people are reluctant to give performance feedback to coworkers, especially to their superiors. When they ask themselves, "What do I have to gain by telling my boss about his development needs?" they struggle for an answer.

Inherent in 360-degree feedback is the use of multiple perspectives. There is strength in numbers. As the old saying goes, "If one person tells you that you remind him of a horse's backside, you can ignore him. If ten people tell you the same thing, you probably ought to get fitted for a saddle." Managers receiving 360-degree feedback can be jarred to attention about their shortcomings by virtue of the joint agreement from their raters.

The other benefit of collecting data from different rater groups (i.e., superiors, peers, and subordinates) is that the participant gets to see a panorama of perceptions, which presents a more complete picture than that afforded by any one person or rater group. For example, in many cases subordinates and peers are in a better position than the boss to evaluate some competencies. Bosses are traditionally used to evaluate performance, but direct reports and peers may be in the best position to give the most meaningful feedback on day-to-day leader behavior.[19] There is ample evidence that managers can improve over time as a result of receiving feedback from coworkers.[44,47] Furthermore, working with a coach can amplify the performance gains associated with feedback.[43]

Other Pieces of Advice

So how can busy managers avoid career derailment? The first step is to recognize that focusing exclusively on strengths to the exclusion of weaknesses is perilous. Lombardo and Eichinger[30] suggested that managers need to concentrate more on certain areas and less on other areas. They suggested gaining strengths in new areas, which includes neutralizing or developing weaknesses. For instance, they argued that managers must be continuous, active learners, and be aware of and admit the mistakes of their pasts; additionally, they must learn from their management experiences so that they can make transitions and deal with novel and challenging situations more effectively. Managers should also focus less on the technical skills that got them promoted early in their careers, and focus more on the leadership skills that will help them advance in the latter stages of their careers. Managers should also be less controlling of their work and of others since managers at higher levels have more ambiguous work. Managers should therefore become more tolerant of ambiguity.[17]

Lombardo and Eichinger had other thoughts and helpful pieces of advice as well. They believed that managers need to change their orientations; managers need to be focused less on being promoted, and focused more on solving problems in their jobs and for their organizations. They need to also control their emotions. Derailed managers have characteristically been emotional volcanoes, showing their highs and lows, anger and frustration to anyone who is around to see. In a related manner, managers need to become aware of their interpersonal impact on others. Managers who derail have been described as leaving a trail of bruised egos in their path up the organization, oftentimes unknowingly. Everything from e-mails, phone calls, presentations, meetings, face-to-face communication, even the nonverbal communication that managers convey all can leave lasting impressions to the intended audience. We fully agree with Hogan and Benson (this volume) that managers need to be aware of their impact on those they work with.

Before we close, it should be noted that derailment does not mean that the manager is beyond hope for the rest of his or her career.[28,40] In fact, there are many success stories of managers who derailed in a previous work environment but went on to find success in a new environment. Derailment is not permanency. Sometimes it was that "lack of fit" in the old company that led to derailment. Managers then left that company and found a new one in which to thrive. If a manager has in fact derailed, he or she needs to take a "career slowdown" and reflect on where he or she is as a manager and as a person; personal growth, development, and learning are key to success.[28] An essential part of this self-assessment is coming to terms with one's strengths *and* one's weaknesses, then creating a plan to accommodate both.

Upshot

In summary, if managers ignore their weaknesses, the odds for personal derailment increase. The good news is that there are things that individuals and organizations can do to lower the odds for derailment.

Managers should:

- Seek feedback throughout their careers on both strengths and weaknesses
- Seek developmental opportunities that can neutralize or overcome weaknesses
- Seek support and coaching prior to and during transitions
- Be aware that new jobs require new perspectives and behaviors

Organizations should:

- Encourage and support zigzagging career paths over vertical ones
- Provide formal feedback systems that provide confidential, accurate, and timely behavioral data
- Give "how you did it" feedback as well as "what you did" feedback
- Avoid considering one failure as "off the track," but instead capitalize on the learning opportunity
- Allow managers to complete their jobs or their assignments before moving them on

Ignoring weaknesses and focusing exclusively on strengths is an invitation to derailment. By following these guidelines, managers can develop over the spans of their careers and prevent their inevitable weaknesses from stalling a promising career.

References

1. Allen, T. D., Freeman, D. M., Russell, J. E. A., Reizenstein, R. C., & Rentz, J. O. (2001). Survivor reactions to organizational downsizing: Does time ease the pain? *Journal of Occupational and Organizational Psychology, 74*, 145-164.

2. Bentz, V. J. (1985, August). *A view of the top: A thirty year perspective of research devoted to the discovery, description and prediction of executive behavior.* Paper presented at the annual meeting of the American Psychological Association, Los Angeles, CA.

3. Berglas, S. (this volume). Victims of their own success.

4. Bray, D. W., Campbell, R. J., & Grant, D. L. (1974). *Formative years in business.* New York: Wiley & Sons.

5. Bray, D. W., & Howard, A. (1983). The AT&T longitudinal studies of managers. In K. W. Shaie (Ed.), *Longitudinal studies of adult psychological development.* New York: The Guilford Press.

6. Bunker, K. A., Kram, K. E., & Ting, S. (2002). The young and the clueless. *Harvard Business Review, 80*, 80-87.

7. Costa, P. T. Jr., & McCrae, R. R. (1994). Longitudinal stability of adult personality. In R. Hogan, J. A. Johnson, & S. R. Briggs (Eds.), *Handbook of personality psychology* (pp. 269-290). San Diego, CA: Academic Press Inc.

8. Costa, P. T. Jr., & McCrae, R. R. (1997). Set like plaster? Evidence for the stability of adult personality. In T. F. Heatherton & J. L. Weinberger (Eds.), *Can personality change?* (pp. 21-40). Washington DC: American Psychological Association.

9. Davies, M. R. (this volume). Unlocking the value of exceptional personalities.

10. Dotlich, D. L., & Cairo, P. C. (2003). W*hy CEOs fail: The 11 behaviors that can derail your climb to the top—and how to manage them.* San Francisco: Jossey-Bass.

11. Eichinger, R. W., Dai, G., & Tang, K. Y. (this volume). It depends upon what you mean by a strength.

12. Finkelstein, S. (2004). *Why smart executives fail.* New York: Portfolio.

13. Finkin, E. F. (1991, March/April). Techniques for making people more productive. *The Journal of Business Strategy, 12*, 53-56.

14. Gabarro, J. J. (1987). *The dynamics of taking charge.* Boston: Harvard Business School Press.

15. Gentry, W. A., Hannum, K. H., Ekelund, B., & de Jong, A. (2007). A study of the discrepancy between self- and observer-ratings on managerial derailment characteristics of European managers. *European Journal of Work and Organizational Psychology, 16*, 295-325.

16. Gillespie, N.A., Walsh, M., Winefield, A. H., Dua, J., & Stough, C. (2001). Occupational stress in universities: Staff perceptions of the causes, consequences, and moderators of stress. *Work & Stress, 15*, 53-72.

17. Hodgson, P., & White, R. (2001). *Relax, it's only uncertainty*. London: Prentice Hall.

18. Hogan, R., & Benson, M. J. (this volume). Personality theory and positive psychology: Strategic self-awareness.

19. Hogan, R., Curphy, G. J., & Hogan, J. (1994). What we know about leadership: Effectiveness and personality. *American Psychologist, 49*, 493-504.

20. Hogan, R., & Hogan, J. (2001). Assessing leadership: A view from the dark side. *International Journal of Selection and Assessment, 9*(1-2), 40-51.

21. Hogan, R., & Kaiser, R. B. (2005). What we know about leadership. *Review of General Psychology, 9*, 169-180.

22. Johnson, W., McGue, M., & Krueger, R. F. (2005). Personality stability in late adulthood: A behavioral genetic analysis. *Journal of Personality, 73*, 523-551.

23. Judge, T. A., LePine, J. A., & Rich, B. L. (2006). Loving yourself abundantly: Relationship of the narcissistic personality to self- and other perceptions of workplace deviance, leadership, and task and contextual performance. *Journal of Applied Psychology, 91*, 762-776.

24. Kaplan, R. E., Drath, W. H., & Kofodimos, J. R. (1985). Do powerful people get less feedback? *Creativity and Innovation Network, 11*(2), 59-65.

25. Katz, D., & Kahn, R. L. (1978). *The social psychology of organizations* (2nd ed.). New York: Wiley.

26. Kotter, J. P. (1982). *The general managers*. New York: The Free Press.

27. Kovach, B. E. (1986). The derailment of fast-track managers. *Organizational Dynamics, 15*, 41-48.

28. Kovach, B. E. (1989). Successful derailment: What fast-trackers can learn while they're off the track. *Organizational Dynamics, 18*, 33-47.

29. Leslie, J. B., & Van Velsor, E. (1995). *A look at derailment today: North America and Europe*. Greensboro, NC: Center for Creative Leadership.

30. Lombardo, M. M., & Eichinger, R. W. (1989/2005). *Preventing derailment: What to do before it's too late*. Greensboro, NC: Center for Creative Leadership.

31. Lombardo, M. M., & McCauley, C. (1988). *The dynamics of managerial derailment*. Greensboro, NC: Center for Creative Leadership.

32. Maccoby, M. (2000). Narcissistic leaders: The incredible pros, the inevitable cons. *Harvard Business Review, 78*(1), 68-78.

33. McCall, M. W., Jr., & Lombardo, M. M. (1983). *Off the track: Why and how successful executives get derailed*. Greensboro, NC: Center for Creative Leadership.

34. McKinley, W., Zhao, J., & Rust, K. G. (2000). Sociocognitive interpretation of organizational downsizing. *Academy of Management Review, 25*, 227-243.

35. Millikin-Davies, M. (1992). *An exploration of flawed first-line supervision*. Unpublished doctoral dissertation, University of Tulsa.

36. Morrison, A, M., White, R. P., & Van Velsor, E. (1987). *Breaking the glass ceiling: Can women reach the top of America's largest corporations?* Reading, MA: Addison-Wesley.

37. Moscoso, S., & Salgado, J. F. (2004). 'Dark side' personality styles as predictors of task, contextual, and job performance. *International Journal of Selection and Assessment, 12*, 356-362.

38. Rogers, R. W., & Smith, A. B. (2004). Spotting executive potential and future senior leaders. *Employment Relations Today, 31* (1), 51-60.

39. Sessa, V. I., Kaiser, R. B., Taylor, J. K., & Campbell R. J. (1998). *Executive selection: A research report on what works and what doesn't.* Greensboro, NC: Center for Creative Leadership.

40. Shipper, F., & Dillard, J. E., Jr. (2000). A study of impending derailment and recovery of middle managers across career stages. *Human Resource Management, 39*, 331-345.

41. Shipper, F., & Wilson, C. L. (1992). The impact of managerial behaviors on group performance, stress, and commitment. In K. E. Clark, M. B. Clark, & D. P. Campbell (Eds.), *Impact of Leadership* (pp. 119-129). Greensboro, NC: Center for Creative Leadership.

42. Smart, B. (1999). *Topgrading: How leading companies win by hiring, coaching, and keeping the best people.* Upper Saddle River, NJ: Prentice Hall.

43. Smither, J. W., London, M., Flautt, R., Vargas, Y., & Kucine, I. (2003). Can working with an executive coach improve multisource feedback ratings over time? A quasi-experimental field study. *Personnel Psychology, 56*, 23-44.

44. Smither, J. W., London, M., & Reilly, R. (2005), Does performance improve following multisource feedback? A theoretical model, meta-analysis, and review of empirical findings. *Personnel Psychology, 58*, 33-66.

45. Sorcher, M. (1985). *Predicting executive success: What it takes to make it into senior management.* New York: Wiley.

46. Van Velsor, E., & Leslie, J. B. (1995) Why executives derail: Perspectives across time and cultures. *Academy of Management Executive, 9*(4), 62-72.

47. Walker, A. G., & Smither, J. W. (1999). A five-year study of upward feedback: What managers do with their results matters. *Personnel Psychology, 52*, 393-423.

48. Wells, S. J. (2005). Diving in. *HR Magazine, 50*, 54-59.

49. White, R. P., & DeVries, D. L. (1990). Making the wrong choice: Failure in the selection of senior-level managers. *Issues & Observations, 10*(l), 1-6.

CHAPTER 8

PERSONALITY THEORY AND POSITIVE PSYCHOLOGY
Strategic Self-Awareness

Robert Hogan
Hogan Assessment Systems

Michael J. Benson
Johnson & Johnson

Is it better to be a dissatisfied Socrates or a satisfied pig?
— Ancient Greek Maxim

Leadership requires balancing a number of competing tensions—for example, focusing on short-term versus long-term results, or focusing on people versus task requirements (for example, see Kaiser & Kaplan, this volume). This chapter concerns a different tension—that between living with oneself and living with others. Using personality psychology as a roadmap, we argue that leadership effectiveness depends more on being able to live with others than with being able to live with oneself. Moreover, being able to live with others depends on a capacity that we call "strategic self-awareness"—understanding one's strengths, abilities, and limitations in relation to other people. Consider the following example.

Narcissistic people are supremely comfortable living with themselves, and they are often found in positions of leadership. As CEOs, they take bold and radical actions and engage in major strategic changes, some of which make no sense.[9] Jean-Marie Messier was the CEO of the Paris-based *Compagnie Generale des Eaux* (CGE) from 1996 to 2001. Those who knew Messier described him as self-absorbed, utterly self-confident, and fond of the spotlight. His company, CGE, was a highly profitable, global leader in water, electrical, and waste utilities, and faced the prospects of steady long-term growth worldwide. Nothing about its environment, staff, or core competencies indicated *any* need for change. With no experience whatsoever in the world of media and entertainment, Messier transformed CGE to a movie and music enterprise that he named Vivendi, a transformation that turned into a total financial disaster.

Positive Psychology in the Context of Personality Psychology

The principle dynamic in every organization is the individual search for power, and the history of organizations (and individual careers) concerns how these searches play out.[22] Thus, personality psychology is at the heart of organizational dynamics and the core of leadership effectiveness. Nonetheless, academic discussions of organizational effectiveness typically ignore personality. In contrast, real managers understand that personality is an important factor in occupational performance, although they get little advice from the academics. This may explain the current enthusiasm for a strengths-based approach to leadership development—it is a personality-based model of occupational effectiveness.

This chapter has two goals. The first is to put positive psychology in the context of personality psychology more broadly considered. The second is to use that context to show that positive psychology presents a limited view of human motivation and leadership effectiveness, particularly because it overlooks the decisive and detrimental impact of weaknesses.

Living with Oneself

Traditional personality psychology began with French and German psychiatry in the late 19th century; it extends through Carl Rogers and Abraham Maslow in the 1950s and 1960s, and is represented today by cognitive behavioral therapy and positive psychology.[52] We call this tradition *intrapsychic theory* because it focuses on processes inside people; it emphasizes self-discovery and maintains that the big problem in life is learning to live with oneself. The underlying assumption of this tradition is that everyone has hidden secrets—these could be strengths or limitations; these secrets need to be revealed and explored so that people can "become whole".

Freud's views regarding the need for self-analysis were interesting. He told his most famous patient, a young woman named Dora, that the goal of psychoanalysis was not to make her happy but rather to persuade her to exchange her neurotic unhappiness for the common misery of mankind. In contrast, positive psychology argues that life is about discovering one's strengths so that one can grow, flourish, and be happy—it is about learning to live with oneself. It is worth noting that learning to live with oneself is, relatively speaking, easier than learning how to live with others.

Living with Others

A second and much less influential tradition in personality psychology is called *interpersonal theory*; it began in 1908 with the great Scottish psychiatrist William McDougall (whose thinking was not influenced by Freud) and extends through G. H. Mead in the 1930s and Irving Goffman and Theodore Sarbin in the 1960s. Interpersonal theory is represented today by socioanalytic theory.[25] This tradition focuses on social interaction and assumes that learning to live with others is more important than learning to live with oneself.

Socioanalytic theory starts with two generalizations: people always live in groups, and every group has a status hierarchy. These generalizations have important implications. For example, they imply that people need attention and social approval and find criticism and rejection stressful. They imply that people need power and the control of resources and find the loss of power and control stressful. We summarize this by saying that the two big problems in life concern "getting along" and "getting ahead". People who have power, status, and social support live longer and are happier than those who lack power, status, and social support.[41] In general, people acquire social acceptance and power during social interactions, most often at work. Therefore, learning to live with others is an important skill to develop.

Social interaction is a skilled performance that is formally identical to any other skilled performance like hockey, golf, and acting. This means that there are individual differences in interpersonal skill, and performance, in principle, can be coached and enhanced. We frame the goals of personal development in terms of career success (social support and occupational status), not subjective well being, because one is a prerequisite for the other. Wealth and success may not bring happiness, but poverty and failure only bring misery. More importantly, interpersonal skill is the key to career success,[24] and the essential feature of interpersonal skill is understanding the needs and desires of other people.

Skilled Performance: An Athletic Metaphor

The athletic metaphor is at the core of our thinking—life is "the game of games," and social interaction is the most consequential game of all. As the song "As Time Goes By" from Casablanca went, "It's still the same old story, a fight for love and glory..." (i.e., social acceptance and status); these goals are pursued in athletic contests, drinking bouts, political campaigns, and careers more generally speaking. Success in the game is defined in terms of power, income, and reputation.

In any skilled activity, people differ in a variety of ways and coaching is often used to enhance strengths and minimize performance issues. There are at least five ways in which social interaction resembles a coachable skilled performance (See Table 1).

Individual differences in talent. Some people are faster, stronger, and better coordinated than others. Similarly, some people are smarter, more creative, more charming, and more leader-like than others. The trick for individual competitors is to determine what their strengths and shortcomings are, *relative to their competition.*[14] This can be accomplished most efficiently through a systematic and valid assessment process, and is the strategic way to construct a career. Later in the chapter we outline a systematic approach to the learning and development process (see the section entitled, *Implications for Leadership Development*).

Individual differences in coachability. Some people are coachable; they are eager for feedback, they listen intently, and then they incorporate the feedback in their practice routines and live performances. Thus, being coachable is an individual strength. On the other hand, some people resent coaching, ignore feedback, and insist on marching to the sound of their own drums. Talented people who simply accept the fact that they are not coachable and try to leverage other strengths put themselves at a serious disadvantage—and are at risk for career derailment.[15]

Ability to be a team player. Some people are able to function as part of a team. They subordinate their own agendas to the goals of the team, they support other players, and generally try to make the team perform better. Other people are "team killers". Despite their talent, their self-centered approach to competition erodes the morale of their team and renders it dysfunctional.[45]

Individual differences in sportsmanship. Some people play by the rules, and uphold the spirit of the game; others cheat and bend the rules to gain competitive advantage. In the short run, cheaters tend to win; in the long run, they tend to fail. Enron was an organization whose culture was defined by cheating, and it experienced fabulous short-term success. Cheating has two causes. On the one hand, some people believe rules only apply to other people; this attitude characterizes psychopaths .[2,3] On the other hand, some people are pathologically ambitious and will do anything to win. In either case, cheaters are self-centered and have no regard for the rights of others and no concern about how their actions impact their teams or organizations.

Ability to perform under pressure. Some people respond well to pressure and elevate their performances, and they do this consistently. Other people respond poorly to pressure, and their performances deteriorate correspondingly. No matter how talented people may be, their ability to handle pressure will ultimately influence their career success. Indeed, losing one's composure is a common cause of career derailment.[39]

Table 1.
Skilled Performance: The Five Coachable Skills.

1	Individual differences in talent
2	Individual differences in coachability
3	Ability to be a team player
4	Sportsmanship
5	Ability to perform under pressure

Strategic Self-Awareness

As noted earlier, the mainstream (and dominant) intrapsychic tradition of personality psychology defines self-knowledge in terms of becoming aware of thoughts and emotions (and strengths) that were formerly unconscious. This is sometimes popularly expressed as getting in touch with one's emotions, strengths, or even one's "inner child." This definition of self-awareness is the cornerstone of traditional psychotherapy, and it would be difficult to overstate how influential it has been. In our view, it is also incorrect, and it takes the process of guided individual development in the wrong direction.

Socrates' maxim was "know thyself;" he also famously maintained that the unexamined life is not worth living. However, Socrates and the ancient Greeks meant something very specific by self-knowledge. They were a practical people and they defined self-knowledge in terms of understanding the limits of one's performance capabilities—that is, knowing one's strengths and shortcomings vis-à-vis one's competitors in various activities. This is a sensible way to think about self-awareness; we refer to it as strategic self-awareness because it is information that can be used to shape and direct one's career. There are two components of strategic self awareness: (1) understanding one's limitations and strengths; and (2) understanding how they compare with those of others. The second part is what distinguishes self-awareness from strategic self-awareness. Three important points must be noted about this model of self-awareness.

First, strategic self-awareness cannot be gained in a vacuum or through introspection. Strategic self-awareness depends on performance-based feedback using a systematic and objective assessment process. If people want to improve their golf games, they will consult a golf pro who will ask them to hit some balls, perhaps video-tape their performance, then offer feedback. If they want to improve their tennis game, they will do the same thing. But what should they do if they want to improve their life (or career) games? They will need feedback on their habitual ways of dealing with other people—that is , the interpersonal moves they typically employ in their efforts to get along and get ahead.

Second, for career success, people need feedback in the five performance areas mentioned above: their talent level in various performance domains, the degree to which they can be coached, their ability to function as part of a team, their sportsmanship, and their ability to perform under pressure. For example, well developed multi-rater tools (360-degree feedback instruments) that contain evaluations from different perspectives can provide insight regarding current performance. The information can then be used to devise a plan to expand one's capabilities (add new skills), expand one's capacity (improve existing skills), and find ways to compensate for shortcomings.

Third, we believe feedback should be framed in terms of three categories: (1) Keep doing—continue doing whatever a person is doing correctly; (2) Stop doing—eliminate troublesome or counterproductive behaviors; (3) Start doing—acquire new behaviors that will enhance a person's performance.

Problems with Accentuating the Positive

In athletics as in life, the only news in good news is that future behavior (or performance) should mimic past behavior—that is, continue doing what one is doing. But persistence does not necessarily lead to growth and improvement(for an illustrative example, see the case study of fallen CEO and founder of Digital Equipment Corporation, Ken Olsen, in chapter 6 by Steven Berglas).[7] Performance only improves if people know what they are doing wrong, and that information only comes from negative feedback.

The most common forms of negative feedback occur via frustration, failure, and defeat. Consider Bill Belichick, the immensely successful coach of the New England Patriots, an American professional football team. In 2007, the Patriots won an unprecedented 18 games in a row. In an interview with the *New York Times*, a star player commented on Belichick's coaching style. At the start of each week of practice he spends 4 or 5 minutes talking about what the team did right in the last game, and 45 minutes talking about what it did wrong. This is how winners in athletics analyze their performance. Once again, the information needed to create or sustain success is not found by patting oneself on the back, rather people need to understand what they do well and should continue doing, then move on to identifying the problems that are likely to cause failure in the future. Further, focusing on what has worked in the past will limit flexibility and responsiveness, especially in global environments characterized by complexity and rapid change.

Moreover, in life, strengths turn into problems and even weaknesses after a point.[42,34,35] Consider the personality characteristic called conscientiousness. Some researchers believe that conscientiousness is the most important personality characteristic driving job performance. Conscientiousness is important in stable environments where consistency is valuable. But conscientious people tend to be rigid and inflexible and they adapt poorly to change. In fact, several researchers report finding curvilinear relationships between conscientiousness and performance, suggesting that increasing levels of conscientiousness improve performance up to a point, after which it becomes a detriment.[11,38,50] Much of this research concerned student and clerical performance, but a study of managers by Benson and Campbell[6] found a similar curvilinear relationship—performance-enhancing characteristics only did so up to a point. Strategic self-awareness would tell high scorers when conscientiousness or other qualities stop being a performance asset and turn into a liability.

Now consider individual differences in the ability to live with oneself. Self-acceptance, self-esteem, feelings of self-worth, positive affectivity, adjustment, and self-confidence are all part of the same general construct which Judge and Bono[29] call "core self-evaluations." People with high scores on measures of core self-evaluation experience positive self-regard and live comfortably with themselves. Modern research reveals several interesting generalizations about this capacity for self-appreciation. First, persons with a strong sense of self-worth are able to handle stress and pressure effectively. Second, a sense of positive self-worth is related to career success in management.[30] Third, a sense of positive self-worth is negatively related to performance in sales; this is because ambitious but self-doubting people are driven to perform, whereas persons with strong feelings of self-worth often lack a sense of urgency. Fourth, persons with high self-esteem typically overestimate their competency and won't listen to feedback,[37] and the same is true for managers.[10]

Lessons for Leadership

Positive psychology has some specific things to say about leadership. The approach known as strengths-based development maintains that management training and development efforts that focus on fixing weaknesses are, at best, misdirected and, more likely, simply wrong.[8,18] Proponents of strengths-based development maintain that it is a mistake to worry about shortcomings because they are so hard to change; it is far better to identify managers' natural inclinations and nurture them. Helping managers maximize their innate gifts will naturally foster and encourage their leadership abilities.

On the one hand, this is essentially a restatement of Maslow's self-actualization theory, a view that was vastly popular in organizational psychology in the 1960s and 1970s. Maslow's theory suffers from three problems. First, it is an effort to import Marxism into psychology—for Marx, the goal of the state is to help each citizen realize his or her own innate potential—and Marxism has been discredited as a theory of economics and history. Second, an innate need for self-actualization makes no sense from the perspective of evolutionary theory—what adaptive advantage is associated with being self-actualized? Can individual differences in self-actualization be observed in chimpanzees? If self-actualization confers no adaptive advantages and is not part of our genetic legacy, then it makes no sense to say it is a fundamental component of human nature. And third, after all these years, we have no good psychometric measures of self-actualization, which further suggests that such a need doesn't exist.

On the other hand, a strengths-based development model doesn't fit the reality of the demands of leadership. Leader (or manager) is a role in an organization just like shortstop is a role on a baseball team. To play the role of shortstop, people must have certain agreed-upon characteristics—good mobility, reflexes, and hand-eye coordination; a strong throwing arm; and the ability to perform under pressure. Similarly, to play the role of leader, people must have certain agreed-upon characteristics. To understand those characteristics, we need first to define leadership.

Defining Leadership

Kaiser, Hogan, and Craig[33] note that in the research literature, leadership is almost always defined in terms of the people who are in charge. And leadership is almost always evaluated using ratings by the people who appointed those people in the first place. The authors then make three points about this definition[33]: first, the people at the top of large organizations (e.g., the U.S. Department of Defense) are always good politicians but only sometimes good leaders; second, the use of this definition is the reason for the conflicting findings so common in leadership research; and third, it is wrong. They then argue that leadership should be defined in terms of the ability to build and maintain high performing teams—because leadership involves getting results through other people—and leadership should be evaluated in terms of the performance of the team vis-à-vis their competitors. This is rarely done, but when it is done, the leadership research begins to make more sense.

Various lines of research converge on the view that four broad categories of skill underlie effective leadership.[26] The first, called *intrapersonal skills*, contains two components that concern managing oneself. The first is core self-esteem,[29] emotional security, or resiliency—the ability to control one's emotions and stay calm under pressure. Core self-esteem is easily assessed using any well-validated measure of emotional stability and these measures predict a wide variety of positive career outcomes, including job satisfaction and performance evaluations.[29] The second component of intrapersonal skills concerns self-control—the ability to manage wayward impulses and desires—and is easily assessed using well-validated personality measures of conscientiousness.[19] These measures predict a wide variety of career outcomes, including supervisors' ratings of performance .[20]

The second category of skill underlying leadership is called *interpersonal skill* and concerns the ability to build and maintain relationships with different people; it is easily measured using well-validated personality measures of extraversion and agreeableness,[5] and these measures predict a wide range of occupational outcomes, including supervisory performance.[23] These skills are essential to establishing and sustaining the relationships needed to build a team. For example, Duffy, Ganster, and Pagon[13] show that unpredictable and inconsiderate leaders alienate their followers and are unable to build and maintain high performing teams and achieve positive organizational results.

The third category of skill underlying leadership is called *technical skills*, and it differs from the preceding two categories in several ways. Technical skills can be taught and don't depend on social skill. Technical skills involve comparing, compiling, analyzing, coordinating, innovating, synthesizing, and so on.[48] They can be assessed using work simulations, assessment center exercises, and content-valid tests; the best predictors of individual differences in technical skills, however, are measures of cognitive ability.[27,49,51] These measures predict supervisor ratings of judgment, market savvy, training progress, and job knowledge.[20] Technical skills are important for leadership because leaders need to seem knowledgeable and competent and act as a resource for the performance of their group.

The fourth category, *leadership skills*, concerns building and maintaining effective teams and can be analyzed in terms of five components (See Table 2)—which depend on intrapersonal, interpersonal, and technical skills.

Leadership Skills

The first component of leadership skills is recruiting talented people to a team. The second component involves retaining talented people once they are recruited. The third component concerns motivating a team. Recruiting, retaining, and motivating team members depends on building positive relationships with each team member, which in turn depends on the interpersonal skills described above. The fourth component concerns developing and promoting a vision for the team, a vision that legitimizes the team enterprise. Technical competence is needed to develop the vision, and interpersonal skills are needed to sell it. The final component concerns being persistent and hard to discourage. Persistence probably depends on self-esteem and conscientiousness, although there is little research on the topic. Leadership skill can be assessed using any number of well-validated procedures, although the most effective assessments use a combination of methods. Recent meta-analyses indicate that measures of cognitive ability and personality substantially predict leadership emergence and effectiveness [28,31,30] and leadership role occupancy.[1]

Table 2.
The Five Critical Areas That Define Leadership Skill in the Domain Model.

1	Recruiting talented people
2	Retaining talented people
3	Motivating a team
4	Developing & promoting a vision
5	Persistence & perseverance

Table 3.
Dimensions of the Dark Side of Personality

Dimension	Definition	As a Strength	As a Shortcoming
Excitable	Mood swings, emotional outbursts, and inability to persist on projects	Empathy and concern	Emotional explosiveness
Skeptical	Mistrusting others, questioning their motives, and challenging their integrity	Social and political insight	Excessive Suspicion
Cautious	Fearful of making mistakes, avoid making decisions, resisting change, using only proven solutions to problems, and alienating their staffs	Evaluates risks appropriately	Indecisiveness and risk aversion
Reserved	Remaining aloof, communicating poorly, and ignoring the welfare of their staffs	Emotionally unflappable	Insensitive and poor communicator
Leisurely	Procrastinating, pursuing their own agendas, and failing to set clear expectations for, or following through with commitments to, their staffs	Good social skills	Passive aggression
Bold	Feeling entitled, not sharing credit for success, blaming their mistakes on others, and not learning from experience, but are fearless about pursuing grand goals	Courage and energy	Overbearing and manipulative
Mischievous	Lying and breaking rules to test the limits, ignoring commitments, and thinking they can talk their way out of any problem	Unafraid of risk	Reckless and deceitful
Colorful	Needing to be the center of attention, so that others can admire them, preoccupied with being noticed, unable to maintain focus, and resist sharing credit	Celebrations and entertainment	Impulsive and distractible
Imaginative	Thinking in eccentric ways, often changing their minds, and making strange decisions	Creativity and vision	Bad ideas
Diligent	Frustrating and disempowering their staffs with micro-management, poor prioritization, and an inability to delegate	Hard work and high standards	Micromanagement
Dutiful	Sucking up to supervisors, unable to deny unrealistic requests, won't stand up for their staffs and burn them out as a result	Corporate citizenship	Indecisiveness

These four categories of skills that underlie effective leadership concern what we call the "bright side" of performance, what we see when people are performing at their best. However, a very interesting literature on managerial derailment has developed over the past few years that can be summarized in terms of three generalizations. The first is that the base rate for managerial failure in corporate America is about 50%,[15] and further, bad managers are the principal cause of stress, absenteeism, and turnover in every organization. Every working adult reports having spent some considerable time working for an "intolerable" boss.[36] More bad managers exist than good ones, and they create substantial, but unnecessary, financial problems for their sponsoring organizations.

The second generalization is that the primary reason managers fail is that they are unable to build effective team;[15] rather they create teams of hostile, resentful time-servers searching for opportunities to leave or to retaliate. These team dynamics reflect the dysfunctional interpersonal strategies of leaders, strategies that violate the trust of followers and disrupt the performance of the team. It is also worth noting that these dysfunctional interpersonal strategies often yield short-term results but fail in the long run.[6,23]

Finally, the reason bad managers are unable to build teams concerns how they treat their subordinates. They alienate their subordinates in certain characteristic ways, which can be classified and measured. Table 3 contains a taxonomy of dysfunctional managerial behaviors, which we call dimensions of "the dark side of personality." Note that each of these dark side dimensions has distinct positive features (listed in Table 3) that are initially attractive and positively related to performance; the problem is one of overdoing.[34] Consider the first dimension, *Excitable*. People with high scores on Excitable approach new projects and people with energy, passion, and enthusiasm—all of which are attractive; the problem is that these people are easily discouraged and lack persistence. The research by Benson and Campbell[6] concerning curvilinear relationships between personality and leadership performance is based partly on the dimensions in Table 3. Note also that these dark side dimensions coexist with the bright side, which means that they are hard to detect in interviews, and only become apparent over time, after people begin to let down their guards and "be themselves". Finally, everyone has some dark side issues, and it is hard to deal with them through selection. Dark side tendencies must be managed through development and coaching programs—they cannot be ignored. In the next chapter, Malcolm Davies[12] provides a particularly useful model for managing dark side tendencies.

Implications for Development

Strategic self-awareness can be developed and is important for career success. However, an effective leadership development process depends on the following elements: (1) it should be systematic; (2) it should be based on valid assessments; (3) it should be seen as a team activity—individuals, coaches, and management must participate, or the process won't succeed. Success in this process is defined by increases in strategic self-awareness, leadership skill, and team and organizational performance. The Development Pipeline® created and used by Personnel Decisions International (PDI) is an example of a leadership development process that emphasizes strategic self-awareness and the role of multiple stakeholders in driving sustainable change.[17] This process is portrayed in Figure 1.

Figure 1.
The PDI Development Pipeline®

Insight:	Do people know what to develop?
Motivation:	Are people willing to invest the time and energy to develop themselves?
Capabilities:	Do people have the skills and knowledge they need?
Real-World Practice:	Do people have the opportunity to use their new skills at work?
Accountability:	Do people internalize their new skills to actually improve performance and results?

Sustained behavioral change depends on increased strategic self-awareness created by feedback on the performance skills (i.e., individual differences in talent, coachability, ability to be a team player, sportsmanship, and ability to perform under pressure) or leadership skills (i.e., recruiting talented people, retaining talented people, motivating a team, developing and promoting a vision, and persistence and perseverance) outlined in the preceding section.[46,47] Following the Development Pipeline® model in Figure 1 from left to right, we can trace the steps in the development process. The first step concerns insight—does a person know what needs to be developed? For example, coachability is an individual difference category that, to some degree, is determined by intrapersonal and interpersonal skills. A well-validated personality assessment can provide insight regarding these skills, and the insight can be used to drive sustainable behavior change to improve coachability. Furthermore, a multi-rater feedback tool can provide information about differences in terms of coachability, being a team player, or performance under pressure.

Table 4 outlines how we translate the framework of individual differences into the domain model skill areas and then into specific measurement tools. Two important considerations should be noted. First, the leadership skill domain area is noticeably absent. As we noted earlier, the underlying components of leadership skill (see Table 2) depend directly on the other three (intrapersonal, interpersonal, and technical) domain areas; therefore, assessment of leadership skill is best viewed as the outcome of the process implied in Table 4. Second, leadership development is best served by implementing a systematic assessment process that employs a broad range of instruments.

Table 4.
Individual Differences, Skill Domain, and Assessment Method

Individual Difference Category	Skill Domain	Assessment Method
Talent	Technical	Cognitive ability Job knowledge tests
Coachability	Intrapersonal Interpersonal	Personality inventories Multi-rater tools
Ability to be a team player	Interpersonal	Personality inventories (especially Dark Side) Multi-rater tools Assessment center simulations
Sportsmanship	Intrapersonal	Personality inventories Motives and values assessment
Ability to perform under pressure	Intrapersonal Technical	Personality inventories multi-rater tools Assessment center job simulations

The second step concerns motivation: are people willing to invest the time and energy needed to develop? Insight and self-awareness (even strategic self-awareness) is irrelevant if people have no desire or motivation to change. The third step concerns capabilities: whether people have the skills and knowledge they need to develop further. The fourth step involves real-world practice: providing people with opportunities to use new skills on the job and in the moment. In the 1980s, the Center for Creative Leadership highlighted the critical role of experience, dealing with hardships, and derailment tendencies as they relate to developing leaders and enhanced leadership ability.[43,44,53] This research provides a foundation for the critical role of experience in the leadership development process. The fifth step concerns accountability: will people use their new skills to improve performance and results? Development is a team activity, and accountability should involve a mix of internal and external checks and balances on the entire process.

The pipeline analogy for describing development is important for two reasons. First, it allows us to identify where, in the development process, growth may be slowed, blocked, or stopped. Unless bottlenecks are identified and fixed, further developmental efforts will fail. The Development Pipeline® model allows individuals and organizations to diagnose what is and is not working, and to design interventions that are more likely to deliver maximum results. If organizations commit to using systematic development processes—ensuring that they are based on well-validated assessments, and defining development as a team activity—they will be able to grow talent and build high performing teams.

Last Thoughts

George Gallup, and especially Donald Clifton, pioneered positive psychology under the banner of "science and the study of strengths." They also developed a substantial research organization to realize their intellectual agenda. There is much to admire about their work. For example, their survey research methodology is exemplary and has produced empirical results linking employee attitudes to business results that are both definitive and important.[16] We especially admire their focus on real business outcomes—for example, profitability, productivity, turnover, and customer satisfaction. We also appreciate the humanism implied by their concern with employee well-being. In addition, Gallup researchers have firmly established that management practices are the key drivers of employee engagement, and employee engagement predicts a host of business results.

Although we admire the way positive psychology focuses on effectiveness and high-level performance, it is important to note three things about this emphasis. First, it is not new. The Institute of Personality Assessment and Research (IPAR) at the University of California, Berkeley was established in 1949, based on a Rockefeller Foundation Grant, explicitly to study the determinants of competence, effectiveness, and high-level performance. Over the years, IPAR researchers have assessed over 2,000 highly effective and creative professionals and published many papers describing their findings. Perhaps the best known of these are papers on the nature of creativity.[4,40]

Second, high-level effectiveness is not the same thing as *flourishing*, a key term for positive Psychology. IPAR data, for example, clearly show that many if not most talented and accomplished people are driven by private demons.

Finally, it is not at all clear what *flourishing* means. If it means satisfaction with oneself, then it is clearly only one aspect of psychological health, and it is an aspect that is closely related to narcissism. As such, it is likely to increase the ability to live with oneself at the expense of the ability to live with others, which in turn, will decrease the probability of occupational success.[32] If *flourishing* means self-actualization as Maslow defined the term, then it is simply wrong-headed.

References

1. Arvey, R. D., Rotundo, M., Johnson, W., Zhang, Z., & McGue, M. (2006). The determinants of leadership role occupancy: Genetic and personality factors. *Leadership Quarterly, 17,* 1-20.

2. Babiak, P. (1995). When psychopaths go to work: A case study of an industrial psychopath.*Applied Psychology, 44,* 171-188.

3. Babiak, P., & Hare, R. D. (2006). *Snakes in suits: When psychopaths go to work.* New York: Reagan Books.

4. Barron, F. X. (1969). *Creative person and creative process.* New York: Holt, Rinehart, and Winston.

5. Bartram, D. (2005). The great eight competencies: A criterion-centric approach to validation. *Journal of Applied Psychology, 90,* 1185-1203.

6. Benson, M. J., & Campbell, J. P. (2007). To be, or not to be, linear: An expanded representation of personality and its relationship to leadership performance. *International Journal of Selection and Assessment, 15*, 232-249.

7. Berglas, S. (this volume). Victims of their own success.

8. Buckingham, M., & Clifton, D. O. (2001). *Now, discover your strengths.* New York: Free Press.

9. Chatterjee, A., & Hambrick, D. C. (2007). It's all about me: Narcissistic CEOs and their effects on company strategy and performance. *Administrative Science Quarterly, 52,* 351-386.

10. Church, A. H. (1997). Managerial self-awareness in high performing individuals in organizations. *Journal of Applied Psychology, 82*, 281-292.

11. Cucina, J. M., & Vasilopoulos, N. L. (2005). Nonlinear personality-performance relationships and the spurious moderating effects of traitedness. *Journal of Personality, 73,* 227-259.

12. Davies, M. R. (this volume). Unlocking the value of exceptional personalities.

13. Duffy, M. K., Ganster, D. C., & Pagon, M. (2002). Social undermining in the workplace. *Academy of Management Journal, 45*, 331-351.

14. Eichinger, R. W., Dai, G., & Tang, K. Y. (this volume). It depends upon what you mean by a strength.

15. Gentry, W. A. & Chappellow, C. T. (this volume). Managerial derailment: Weaknesses that can be fixed.

16. Harter, J. K., Schmidt, F. L., & Hayes, T. L. (2002). Business-unit-level relationship between employee satisfaction, employee engagement, and business outcomes: A meta-analysis. *Journal of Applied Psychology, 87*, 268-279.

17. Hicks, M. D., & Peterson, D. B. (1999). The development pipeline: How people really learn. *Knowledge Management Review, 2*, 30-33.

18. Hodges, T. D., & Clifton, D. O. (2004). Strengths-based development in practice. In P. A. Linley & S. Joseph (Eds.), *Positive psychology in practice* (pp. 256-268). Hoboken, NJ: Wiley.

19. Hogan, J., & Hogan, R. (1989). How to measure employee reliability. *Journal of Applied Psychology*, *74*, 273-279.

20. Hogan, J., & Holland, B. (2003). Using theory to evaluate personality and job performance relations: A socioanalytic perspective. *Journal of Applied Psychology*, *88*, 100-112.

21. Hogan, R. (2005). In defense of personality measurement: New wine for old whiners. *Human Performance*, *18*, 331-341.

22. Hogan, R. (2007). *Personality and the fate of organizations.* Mahway, NJ: Lawrence Erlbaum.

23. Hogan, R., & Hogan, J. (2001). Assessing leadership: A view from the dark side. *International Journal of Selection and Assessment*, *9*, 40-51.

24. Hogan, R., & Hogan, J. (2002). Leadership and sociopolitical intelligence. In R. E. Riggio, S. E. Murphy, & F. J. Pirozzolo (Eds.), *Multiple intelligences and leadership* (pp. 75-88). San Francisco: Jossey-Bass.

25. Hogan, R., & Smither, R. (2001). *Personality: Theories and applications.* Boulder, CO: Westview Press.

26. Hogan, R., & Warrenfeltz, R. W. (2003). Educating the modern manager. *Academy of Management Learning and Education*, *2*, 74-84.

27. Hunter, J. E., & Hunter, R. F. (1984). Validity and utility of alternative predictors of job performance. *Psychological Bulletin, 96,* 72-98.

28. Ilies, R., Gerhardt, M. W., & Le, H. (2004). Individual differences in leadership emergence: Integrating meta-analytic findings and behavioral genetics estimates. *International Journal of Selection and Assessment*, *12*, 207-219.

29. Judge, T. A., & Bono, J. E. (2001). Relationship of core self-evaluations traits—self esteem, generalized self-efficacy, locus of control, and emotional stability—with job satisfaction and job performance. *Journal of Applied Psychology*, *86*, 80-92.

30. Judge, T. A., Bono, J. E., Ilies, R., & Gerhardt, M. W. (2002). Personality and leadership: A qualitative and quantitative review. *Journal of Applied Psychology*, *87*, 765-780.

31. Judge, T. A., Colbert, A. E., & Ilies, R. (2004). Intelligence and leadership: A quantitative review and test of theoretical propositions. *Journal of Applied Psychology*, *89*, 542-552.

32. Judge, T. A., LePine, J. A., & Rich, B. L. (2006). Loving yourself abundantly: Relationship of the narcissistic personality to self-and other perceptions of workplace deviance, leadership, and task and contextual performance. *Journal of Applied Psychology, 91*, 762-776.

33. Kaiser, R. B., Hogan, R., & Craig, S. B. (2008). Leadership and the fate of organizations. *American Psychologist, 63*, 96-110.

34. Kaiser, R. B., & Kaplan, R. E. (this volume). When strengths run amok.

35. Kaplan, R. E., & Kaiser, R. B. (in press). Towards a positive psychology for leaders. In P. A. Linley, S. Harrington, & N. Page (Eds.), *Oxford Handbook of Positive Psychology and Work.* New York: Oxford University Press.

36. Kellerman, B. (2004). *Bad leadership: What it is. How it happens. Why it Matters.* Boston: Harvard Business School Press.

37. Kruger, J., & Duning, D. (1999). Unskilled and unaware of it: How difficulties in recognizing one's own incompetence lead to inflated self-assessments. *Journal of Personality and Social Psychology*, *77*, 1121-1134.

38. LaHuis, D. M., Martin, N. R., & Avis, J. M. (2005). Investigating nonlinear conscientiousness-job performance relations for clerical employees. *Human Performance, 18,* 199-212.

39. Lombardo, M. M., Ruderman, M. N., & McCauley, C. D. (1988). Explanations of success and derailment in upper-level management positions. *Journal of Business and Psychology, 2,* 199-216.

40. MacKinnon, D. W. (1962). The nature and nurture of creative talent. *American Psychologist*, *17*, 484-495.

41. Marmot, M. (2004). *The status syndrome.* New York: Times Books.

42. McCall, M. W., Jr. (this volume). Every strength a weakness and other caveats.

43. McCall, M. W., Jr., & Lombardo, M. (1983). Off the track: Why and how successful executives get derailed (Tech. Rep. No. 21). Greensboro, NC: Center for Creative Leadership.

44. McCall, M. W., Jr., Lombardo, M., & Morrison, A. (1988). *Lessons of experience: How successful executives develop on the job.* New York: Free Press.

45. Peeters, M. A. G., Van Tuijl, H. F. J. M., Rutte, C. G., & Reymen, I. M. M. J. (2006) Personality and team performance: A meta-analysis. *European Journal of Personality*, *20*, 377-396.

46. Peterson, D. B., & Hicks, M. D. (1995). *Leader as coach: Strategies for coaching and development.* Minneapolis, MN: Personnel Decisions International.

47. Peterson, D. B., & Hicks, M. D. (1996). *Development FIRST: Strategies for self-development.* Minneapolis, MN: Personnel Decisions International.

48. Peterson, N. G., Mumford, M. D., Borman, W. C., Jeanneret, P. R., & Fleishman, E. A. (1999). *An occupational information system for the 21st century: The development of the O*NET.* Washington, DC: American Psychological Association.

49. Ree, M. J., & Earles, J. A. (1992). Intelligence is the best predictor of job performance. *Current Directions in Psychological Science, 1,* 86-89.

50. Robie, C., & Ryan, A.M. (1999). Effects of nonlinearity and heteroscedasticity on the validity of conscientiousness in predicting overall job performance. *International Journal of Selection and Assessment, 7,* 157-169.

51. Schmidt, F. L., & Hunter, J. E. (1998). The validity and utility of selection methods in personnel psychology: Practical and theoretical implications of 85 years of research findings. *Psychological Bulletin, 124,* 262-274.

52. Seligman, M. E. P., & Czikszentmihalyi, M. (2000). Positive psychology: An introduction. *American Psychologist, 55,* 5-14.

53. Van Velsor, E., & Leslie, J. B. (1995). Why executives derail: Perspectives across time and cultures. *Academy of Management Review, 9,* 62-72.

CHAPTER 9

UNLOCKING THE VALUE OF EXCEPTIONAL PERSONALITIES

Malcolm R. Davies
Learning At Work

Introduction

Leadership talent is a scarce commodity and the prevalence of dysfunctional leadership is high.[10] However, individual leaders are not invariably good or invariably bad; as McCall[32] put it in chapter 4, each leader is a tapestry of strengths and weaknesses. The trouble with derailment is not just the poor performance that precedes it, but also that the talent and potential bound up with the derailed leader's troubling qualities get thrown out like the proverbial "baby with the bathwater."

I believe that outstanding leadership is a function of capability, which is influenced by experience and extraordinary personality characteristics. Extraordinary personalities are a mixed blessing, with both assets and liabilities. The challenge guiding my work the last 20 years has been the problem of unlocking the value in exceptional personalities whilst mitigating their potential downside. In this chapter, I provide my solution for retaining the clean baby while draining the dirty water. Although the last two chapters have clearly made the case that weaknesses matter, I hope to show how certain weaknesses can be converted into highly desirable strengths.

Take the case of Carol, a brilliant manager with a large financial services organization. Since obtaining her basic accounting qualification, Carol had worked her way steadily through the ranks, completing graduate studies as she climbed the ladder. In her mid-thirties Carol was appointed as general manager of a substantial state-based operation. A number of exceptional personality characteristics had separated Carol from more experienced, and mostly male, colleagues, resulting in her promotion. These characteristics were her indefatigable drive, her prodigious capacity for work, her attention to microscopic detail, and her capacity to be the life of any gathering.

I had previously met Carol when she studied leadership with me much earlier in her career. It was only weeks into her new role when she called me in for coaching assistance. Results were not meeting expectations, and she was receiving critical feedback from her boss and others. It seemed to her that the skill-set that had brought her success earlier in her career was now troublesome. The pressure was greater, relationships with powerful colleagues were not progressing, her normal ways of venting were no longer working, and the workload was overwhelming her capacity to cope. She was taunted by the Peter Principle and privately thought that she had indeed been promoted to her level of incompetence.

Had her situation continued, Carol may have failed in that role. Major public failure could have been life-changing; she may have left that organization and retreated to a more modest role elsewhere, her talent lost forever. But that did not happen. Instead she was able to develop new insights into the double-edged sword of her talent. She did well in that state-based role and is now in a much larger international role with the same organization. How and why all that happened is the subject of this chapter.

Leadership Capability

I define leadership as the capable use of a set of learnable skills to influence oneself and others to set aside purely personal interests to contribute to the achievement of group goals.[17,20,27] Four important issues are implicit in this definition. First, the key is ability to influence. Leaders influence thought by provoking new ideas; they influence motivation by inducing compliance and inspiring commitment; they influence action by assigning roles and responsibilities, and so on. Second, a person does not have to be a top executive to be a leader. It is important that every manager leads at his or her level. Third, leaders are not simply born; inherent talent must be refined through learning and development. Everyone can learn to be a better leader, and some can learn to be a truly outstanding leader—but it requires focus, dedication, and sustained effort. The fourth issue is the significance of the word *capable*.

Capability

Capability is manifested in effectiveness under pressure. Knowing what to do to be a leader does not mean that a person *can* lead. Knowing how to lead does not mean that a person *will* lead, especially in tough situations. Skilled incompetence is epidemic, hence the prevalence of flawed leadership—and this despite prodigious amounts of management training and development. Capability, as the term is used here, means the ability and motivation to perform skillfully, consistently, and persistently under difficulty or even great duress. Capability is what separates outstanding leaders from the rest.

Many authors have identified exceptional CEOs. Books, articles, and weblogs abound on this topic.[31,6] Qualities described variously as mental toughness, emotional resilience, courage under duress, capacity to persist in the face of large obstacles, and the like, are often mentioned to describe these leadership luminaries. Biographies of these people reveal early evidence for the presence of exceptional personality characteristics. In some ways, none of these leaders is an average human being. If capability is what outstanding leaders have more of, and if knowledge and skill and ability are not sufficient for capability, then it is important to identify the motivational basis for their exquisite capability.

Motivational Basis of Capability

Hogan and Kaiser[20] argue that two sides of leader personality should be distinguished, sides they call the "bright side" and the "dark side." According to them, "the bright side concerns the initial impression we make on others—it reflects our social performance when we are at our best.... The dark side reflects the impression we make on others when we let our guard down or when we are at our worst."[19] Hogan and Hogan[17] argue that the standard personality disorders described in the fourth edition of the *Diagnostic and Statistical Manual of Mental Disorders*[1] provide a taxonomy of dark side personality characteristics, also referred to as derailment factors or *derailers*. The DSM-IV model is a categorization of personality disorders that emerged from a disease-based clinical view. It holds that personality disorders are distinct from normal, bright-side personality factors like the "Big Five" (Extraversion, Agreeableness, Conscientiousness, Stability, and Openness). Whilst normal personality factors are correlated with leadership effectiveness,[23] dark side factors have been linked with leader performance risks and derailment.[16,2,18,14,21] Hogan and Kaiser[20] claim that the dark side has initial appeal, but becomes counterproductive over time: the narcissist's confidence turns into arrogance, the borderline's passion recedes into explosiveness, the avoidant's unflappable resolve becomes indifference to other people's needs, and so on.

Reframing previous interpretations of dark side research, I propose that these characteristics are actually a *source* of success. After all, so-called dark side characteristics are common among effective leaders. In a survey of successful Australian CEOs, Hogan[15] found that every CEO had at least two or three standout dark side factors, potential derailers that needed to be managed. Thus, the dark side is a double-edged sword, motivating exceptional levels of capability, but also potentially leading to counterproductive behavior in the unprepared leader. Because these characteristics have a Jekyll-and-Hyde quality, and because of the high value of the positive side, I do not believe they should be referred to as dark side characteristics, or worse still, personality disorders.

Instead, I refer to dark side or so-called "disordered" personal qualities as *exceptional personality characteristics*. This emphasizes their positive potential and avoids demonization of those who carry them. There is ample evidence to support my claim that exceptional personality is an important source of capability as well as a risk factor. As businesspeople know, the higher the potential return, the higher the risk.

Exceptional Personality

To capitalize on the potential of an exceptional personality and manage the associated risks, we need to understand where it comes from and how to assess it in the workplace.

Origins

Karen Horney's extension of Freudian theory offers a clear model of how exceptional personality characteristics develop and how they ignite such strong drive and motivation. Much of this section is based around brilliant insights published in chapter two of Horney's[22] classic book, *Neurosis and Human Growth*.

Despite wide variation in the quality of childhood parenting or caregiving that people experience, virtually no one has an upbringing completely free of stress or even trauma. Trauma in childhood affects different people in different ways and to different degrees. Some children fail to develop normal feelings of belonging and attachment. Instead they develop vague feelings of insecurity and apprehensiveness, feelings which Horney[22] refers to as "basic anxiety." Once these feelings develop, the child must learn to deal with them. Horney identified three basic patterns of coping with basic anxiety: moving towards others (comply), against others (compete), or away from others (withdraw).

Everyone moves towards, away, and against others to some degree as part of normal functioning, but intense basic anxiety can exaggerate their use. The degree to which an individual's use of these coping strategies departs from normal is directly related to the level of basic anxiety he or she feels. Over time, departures from normal functioning habituate and become enduring features of the individual's personality. They become the individual's default ways of dealing with life. This renders certain behaviors, attitudes, and skills unavailable for use, stimulating a deep need to bolster self confidence to compensate. That need instills a strong drive to prove one's worth, what Horney[22] refers to as a "search for glory."

How the drive manifests itself is shaped by individual predisposition, the nature of the trauma experienced, and so on. For a reasonably small percentage of the population, the drive is too strong, leading to what psychiatrists call personality disorder. For the majority, however, I propose that it is this deep inner drive that affords some individuals the uncommon levels of persistence and tenacity that underlie the motivational component of capability. In other words, for the majority, the end result is an exceptional personality. I further propose that this deep inner drive motivates people to attain success in spheres of activity as diverse as business, military, politics, sports, and the arts.

Assessment

It is one thing to have a theory, it's quite another to do something practical about it. Toward that end, we need a way to measure exceptional personality. Clinical categorization approaches in the personality disorder tradition have been criticized as unscientific and unreflective of true underlying symptoms.[28] Moreover, they are designed for a distressed psychiatric population, which makes them inappropriate in the corporate world. Hogan and Hogan[18] have met the need for a corporate-friendly scientific measurement and classification system of exceptional personality with the creation of the *Hogan Development Survey* (HDS). Drawing inspiration from personality disorder concepts as they may manifest themselves in a work environment, the HDS provides a robust measure of a range of exceptional personalities common among high functioning individuals in a format that is palatable to senior managers. Table 1 contrasts definitions of 11 personality disorders with definitions of 11 HDS factors.

The HDS questionnaire was developed expressly for the workplace. It measures 11 personality factors, referred to as dark side factors or derailers, based on a manager's responses to 168 items concerning typical thoughts, feelings, and behaviors. The HDS may also be taken as part of a suite of measures including bright side personality and motives and value profiles that together provide a comprehensive view of personality. Table 2 lists how each factor may manifest in both positive and negative leadership behavior. Further, Table 2 shows how the factors fit with Horney's[22] three general ways of coping with basic anxiety: moving towards (comply), against (compete), or away (withdraw) from others.

A nine-page statistical and narrative report is one of several optional reports that can be generated to interpret HDS results. That report provides scores on each of the 11 factors presented graphically in percentiles based on norms. Figure1 provides an example of how the overall profile of scores is reported. The report also provides a narrative interpretation of each score. HDS scores that are greater than the 90th percentile give a strong indication of the presence of an exceptional personality factor; scores greater than the 70th percentile give a

Table 1.
DSM Personality Disorder Characteristics and HDS Factor Themes.

Personality disorder	DSM-IV definition	HDS theme	HDS definition
Borderline	A pattern of instability in interpersonal relationships, self-image, and affects, and marked impulsivity.	Excitable	Moody and hard to please; intense but short-lived enthusiasm for people, projects, or things
Paranoid	A pattern of distrust and suspiciousness such that others' motives were interpreted as malevolent.	Skeptical	Cynical, distrustful, and doubting others' true intentions.
Avoidant	A pattern of social inhibition, feelings of inadequacy, and hypersensitivity to negative evaluation.	Cautious	Reluctant to take risks for fear of being rejected or negatively evaluated.
Schizoid	A pattern of detachment from social relationships and a restricted range of emotional expression.	Reserved	Aloof, detached, and uncommunicative; lacking interest in or awareness of the feelings of others.
Passive Aggressive[a]	A pattern of passive resistance to adequate social and occupational performance; irritated when asked to something he/she does not want to do.	Leisurely	Independent; ignoring people's requests and becoming irritated or argumentative if they persist.
Narcissistic	A pattern of grandiosity, need for admiration, and lack of empathy.	Bold	Unusually self-confident; feelings of grandiosity and entitlement; over-evaluations of one's capabilities.
Antisocial	A pattern of disregard for, and violation of, the rights of others.	Mischievous	Enjoying risk taking and testing the limits; needing excitement; manipulative, deceitful, cunning and exploitive.
Histrionic	A pattern of excessive emotionality and attention seeking.	Colorful	Expressive, animated, and dramatic; wanting to be noticed and needing to be the centre of attention.
Schizotypal	A pattern of acute discomfort in close relationships, cognitive or perceptual distortions, and eccentricities of behaviour.	Imaginative	Acting and thinking in a creative and sometimes odd or unusual ways.
Obsessive Compulsive	A pattern of preoccupation with orderliness, perfectionism, and control	Diligent	Meticulous, precise, and Perfectionistic; inflexible about rules and procedures; critical of others' performance.
Dependent	A pattern of submissive and clinging behaviour related to an excessive need to be taken care of.	Dutiful	Eager to please and reliant on others for support and guidance; reluctant to take independent action or go against popular opinion.

Note: All definitions are from the DSM-IV except Passive Aggressive. [a]Passive aggressive definition is from the DSM-III-R. HDS definitions are paraphrased from Hogan, R., and Hogan, J. (1997). *Hogan Development Survey Manual*. Tulsa, OK: Hogan Assessment Systems.

moderate indication. While every individual is different, in general, in my experience, both moderate and strong indications underwrite a degree of individual capability. This capability can underwrite individual talent and success provided that individuals learn to avoid the Icarus Paradox.[33] That is, overuse of a strength, turning that strength into a weakness, as discussed in chapter 4[15] and chapter 5.[11]

Figure1.
Sample of overall summary results from the HDS feedback report

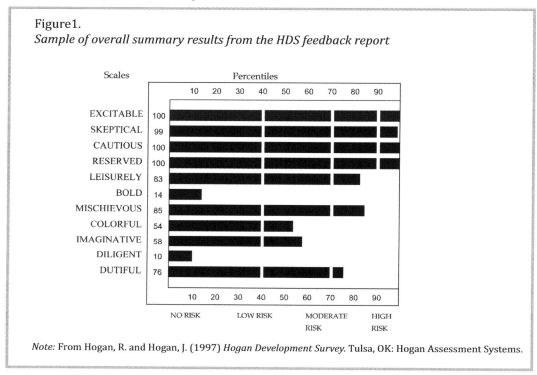

Note: From Hogan, R. and Hogan, J. (1997) *Hogan Development Survey.* Tulsa, OK: Hogan Assessment Systems.

For me, a downside of the current report format is the inherently negative wording used to characterize people with high scores. Unaddressed, this can cause people to dismiss the findings and ignore developmental implications. Most research with the HDS has focused on the downsides of so-called dark side characteristics, whereas my practical use of the test focuses on unlocking the potential in exceptional personality characteristics. Despite this limitation, the HDS offers an excellent vehicle for use in corporate environments. When I reframe the report as being about strong drives and exceptional qualities, most managers have responded well to the discussion and coaching around the idea of minimizing downside tendencies and maximizing the value of their drives.

The Value of Exceptional Personalities

There is plenty of direct and indirect support for the idea of exceptional personality being a source of capability, albeit in the form of a double-edged sword.

Exceptional People for Exceptional Times

Human communities have always had a need for people with very strong drives to do tough jobs like leadership. History is the story of important, if not exceptional, leaders with very strong drives and a tough nature. However, some portion of people with exceptional personalities do not cope well with basic anxiety and the search for glory. These people may come to the attention of clinical and criminal systems, or rise to high office and tyrannically abuse their power and post. Yet history shows that exceptional personality is not all bad news. Some exceptional personalities break the status quo and move their constituents

Table 2.
Best and Worst Characteristics of Managers Scoring High on HDS Exceptional Personality Categories

HDS factor	Best characteristics (Source of capability)	Worst characteristics (Source of derailment)	Coping orientation (Horney, 1950)
Excitable	Great capacity for empathy Know life is not always fair Can feel others' pain Enthusiastic and work hard on new projects	Require constant reassurance Hard to please Change jobs and relationships frequently Easily disappointed	Away
Skeptical	Bright, thoughtful, perceptive Visionary and charismatic Persistent, don't give up without a fight Insightful about organisation politics Good intelligence about others' ideas Passionate commitment to their world views	Expect to be wronged See world as a dangerous place Specialise in conspiracy theories Alert for signs of mistreatment - inevitably find some Retaliate openly when find it	Away
Cautious	Prudent, careful and meticulous at evaluating risk Rarely make ill advised moves Provide sound prudential advice Good counterfoil for impulsive entrepreneurial types	Avoid innovation, resist change Threatened by the new Reactive rather than proactive Rely on the tried and true Very controlling with staff to avoid embarrassment	Away
Reserved	Tough in the face of political adversity Can take criticism, rejection, opprobrium Stay focused in tumult and stress	Ignore needs, moods, feelings of others Rude, tactless, insensitive Isolate from extreme pressure Become unilateral and non-communicative	Away
Leisurely	Good social skills Clever at hiding their feelings Confident about own skills and abilities	Cynical of others' skills and abilities Work at own pace Passively then aggressively resist attempts to change them Need respect and covertly retaliate when they think they don't get it	Away

(Table continues)

143

Table 2. (Cont.)

Bold	Liked, admired, respected by others Energetic, charismatic, leader-like Take the initiative Expect success	Sense of entitlement, overbearing, demanding Excessive self esteem, Arrogant Narcissistic rage when things don't succeed Take most credit for success	Against
Mischievous	Self confident to invulnerability Daring charming, fun, engaging, courageous Handle stress and heavy workloads well	Expect others to like them Expect to extract favours Others are to be exploited Problems maintaining commitments, easily bored Impulsive, reckless, faithless, remorseless, manipulative, don't learn from experience	Against
Colorful	Have flair, dress well, have presence Perform well interpersonally, Fun Good sales people Bright, colourful, entertaining Become busy and enjoy pressure	Call attention to themselves Make dramatic entrances Impulsive and unpredictable Don't listen, don't plan, self promote Sizzle may substitute for substance	Against
Imaginative	Have different perspectives on things Constantly alert for new ways of seeing things Enjoy entertaining others with new ideas Bright, colourful, insightful, imaginative, innovative, creative Insightful about others' motives	Eccentric, odd, flighty Distractible, unpredictable as managers Confuse others because change so often Communicate in unusual ways Self absorbed, Insensitive to others Indifferent to social and political consequences	Against
Diligent	Concerned with doing a good job, pleasing others, obeying authority Hard working, planful, meticulous Set high standards for self and others, reliable Conservative, detail oriented Good organisational citizens, Good role models Popular with bosses	Irritated when rules not followed Nit picking, micro-managing, fussy, deprive subordinates of control Obsessive concern for quality causes problems and stress, Poor at delegating Don't often see the vision or big picture Bottle neck to productivity because everything must pass through them	Towards
Dutiful	Demonstrate service, loyalty, politeness, cordiality Conforming, eager to please, make few enemies	Deeply concerned with being accepted especially by authority figures Alert for signs of disapproval Use every means to ingratiate themselves Do anything the boss requires so tend to be promoted, Staff feel unsupported Indecisive, won't take a stand	Towards

Note: Based on descriptions in work published by Robert Hogan and Joyce Hogan.[18,19]

forward. Dysfunctional individuals aside, I believe that the majority of people who carry exceptional personality can and do remain functional.

Introducing the book *The Structure of Personality*,[11] Professor Carl Lloyd discusses the personality theme of the book by quoting research conducted by the US Navy in the 1990s. The research suggested that candidates best equipped for crewing nuclear submarines evidenced three distinct personality disorders: obsessive-compulsive, schizoid, and avoidant (HDS factors Diligent, Reserved, and Cautious, respectively). Those disorders were regarded as personal strengths in the demanding context of safely running nuclear powered and armed submarines. Crew members need to be preoccupied with orderliness, perfectionism, and control; be socially independent; and be able to function in total isolation. Lloyd concluded that whether a personality attribute is "ordered" or "disordered" is merely a reflection of how well it matches contextual requirements.[11]

Lloyd's insight allowed me to reframe aspects of biographical material of notably good and bad leaders from social, political, military and business contexts such as those profiled in best-selling publications by Gardner[9] and Collins.[5] By analyzing these biographies, I found leader character and behavior descriptions like the characteristics in Table 1. Since the context of senior organizational leadership is a very demanding one, I wondered if Lloyd's lesson about effective submariners might also apply to executives.

Top managers must withstand inordinate pressure, what Levinson[29] called "senior pressure." Senior pressure is created by fast-paced and complex challenges, high ambiguity and uncertainty, expectations to cut costs and increase returns, demands to move faster and outfox the competition while not becoming a takeover target, and so on. Levinson argued that senior pressure demands certain personality characteristics, characteristics that he further argued may be different from those required for success at lower levels. Hambrick, Finkelstein, and Mooney[12] assert that senior job demands may be great, indeed indicating the need for exceptional individuals who can cope with those demands. However, according to Hogan, pressure also influences the expression of dark side personality characteristics, meaning that senior pressure may "bring out a person's worst." Herein lies the dilemma: senior pressure calls for the extraordinary potential in exceptional personalities, but senior pressure may also elicit their destructive potential.

Common at the Top

Intelligent people with strong drive get ahead. They progress up hierarchies because they continuously invest more of what it takes than people with lesser drive. Therefore the prevalence of exceptional personalities should increase as we ascend achievement and success hierarchies in any field of human endeavor including management. Several direct and indirect lines of evidence attest to this phenomenon.

The management psychoanalyst Michael Macoby[31] claims that narcissistic leaders (HDS factor Bold) offer the possibility of "incredible pros and inevitable cons." He argues that, at their best, Bold leaders can be charismatic, visionary, competitive, risk-taking, and creative strategists. Their confidence allows them to build in the face of what can seem impossible odds and emerge in times of discontinuous change to inspire others and create new futures. Macoby offers notable examples, mostly high-tech leaders, such as Andy Grove, Bill Gates, Steve Jobs, Larry Ellison, and Jeff Bezos. Macoby further argues that the downsides he refers to are inevitable. This is where I depart from conventional wisdom with my reframing of exceptional personality and associated developmental activity. For the majority of those with exceptional personality-based drive, the potential cons are not, I believe, necessarily inevitable. I do believe that the majority of successful managers have one or more exceptional personality characteristics at the moderate or strong level.

Board and Fritzon[3] surveyed 39 successful senior business leaders from reputable companies based in the United Kingdom. The authors measured personality disorders using a clinical test. They compared average personality disorder scores for the successful executives with the averages for three clinical samples: psychopaths, criminal mentally ill, and clinical psychiatric patients. The researchers found that the business leaders scored higher on the histrionic personality disorder (HDS Colorful) than the comparison samples; that the leaders' scores for narcissistic personality disorder (HDS Bold) and obsessive-compulsive personality disorder (HDS Diligent) were not significantly different from the three clinical groups; and that the executives had lower scores on the other eight personality disorders. Board and Fritzon further point out that many of the dysfunctional behaviors associated with personality disorders differ only in degree from those valued in senior executives. For instance, Hogan and Hogan[18] state that high scorers on HDS Colorful (DSM-IV histrionic) are often described as talkative (communicative), assertive (leader-like), creative (promote change and new ideas), drawn to crises (likes change), self-promoting (visionary), and intuitive (decisive). This adds considerable weight to the argument that exceptional personality characteristics are common among successful executives. It may be why Hogan and Kaiser argue "low scores on personality disorders are not necessarily desirable" for leaders.[20] I go further and assert that high scores are associated with high performance *for leaders who have learned to manage their drives.*

Based on HDS results for 55 CEOs in Australia, a local CEO network organization called *The Executive Connection* (TEC) found that, "Most CEOs have at least two or three potential derailers [exceptional personality characteristics], which, if well managed, can be great strengths, but if not well managed, can derail people, relationships, and performance."[15] Summary data is presented in the first two columns in Table 3. My review of this study revealed that 93% of the CEOs had at least one moderate exceptional personality characteristic, and 69% had a least one strong exceptional personality characteristic.

Davies[7] surveyed 206 middle- and senior managers in an Australian organization using the HDS. Summary data is a presented in columns 3 and 4 of Table 3. The proportion of those scoring in the high region on a given HDS factor varied between 6% and 41% of the sample for each of the 11 HDS factors and for the moderate region varied between 19% and 73%. Every manager in this sample had a least one exceptional personality characteristic at the moderate level, and 83% of them had at least one at the high level.

Finally, data from 117 upper-middle- to senior mangers attending six recent leadership development programs are presented in the last 2 columns of Table 3. Prevalence of moderate exceptional personality characteristics varied between 21% and 67%, while strong exceptional personality characteristics varied between 8% and 36%. Ninety-nine percent of this sample had at least one moderate exceptional personality characteristic, while 82% had at least one strong exceptional personality characteristic.

The data in Table 3 show that almost all senior executives have at least one moderate or strong exceptional personality characteristic. I propose that the successful managers included in these studies are successful because of strong drives emanating from exceptional personality characteristics. Granted, exceptional personality characteristics may sometimes be a mixed blessing, but they also can be managed positively, allowing deep inner drive to underwrite the focus, persistence, and effort that define exemplary leadership

Table 3.
Prevalence Rates of Exceptional Personality Characteristics

	Sample 1		Sample 2		Sample 3	
Level of EPC[a]	*Moderate*	*High*	*Moderate*	*High*	*Moderate*	*High*
Excitable	37%	15%	54%	29%	41%	27%
Skeptical	61%	15%	57%	16%	40%	12%
Cautious	41%	10%	73%	37%	67%	23%
Reserved	46%	24%	69%	41%	60%	36%
Leisurely	54%	20%	62%	30%	56%	20%
Bold	32%	10%	27%	9%	35%	11%
Mischievous	59%	19%	49%	18%	51%	15%
Colorful	53%	27%	34%	15%	37%	22%
Imaginative	71%	15%	48%	19%	56%	22%
Diligent	22%	7%	19%	10%	21%	9%
Dutiful	12%	0%	26%	6%	27%	8%
At least one EPC[b]	93%	69%	100%	83%	99%	82%

Note: The figures in the table indicate the percentage of managers in each sample who had a moderate (70th percentile or higher) or high (90th percentile or higher) score on the exceptional personality characteristic (as measured by the HDS).
[a] EPC indicates Exceptional Personality Characteristics (defined by the 11 scales on the HDS).
[b] "At least one EPC" values are the percentage of subjects having an elevated score on at least one of the 11 EPCs (HDS scales).
Sample 1 includes the 55 CEOs from the TEC Study;[15] sample 2 includes 206 middle- and senior Australian organization managers;[7] and sample 3 includes 117 upper-middle to senior mangers attending six leadership development programs.

The Downsides are not Inevitable

Most successful executives have at least one exceptional personality characteristic; many have two, three, or even eight. I argue that, in the majority of cases, these characteristics underwrite leadership talent without ever appearing to cause a problem. That talent is a basis for individual and organizational success. Screening people out from selection or promotion because of these characteristics is in my view unwise. You may well screen out the very people your organization needs to thrive in this ever more competitive global economy. Screening is based on the belief that existence of these characteristics is always likely to be bad. I challenge this belief. It is true that some of those with exceptional personality characteristics may find themselves in difficulties related to their drive. In my experience, these people can respond very well to focused development.

Whether they are having problems or not, all managers with exceptional personality characteristics may benefit from development. Carol, the talented woman mentioned at the start of this chapter, had eight moderate to high scores on the HDS. Her talent originates from her very strong drive across a range of areas. Each area has potential downsides, but the downsides are not inevitable. Carol was able to learn how to contain and redirect potentially negative energy towards positive outcomes. This level of success may not be possible for every exceptional personality in every situation, but it is worth the effort to try. More importantly, it is a terrible waste of talent to screen these people out or, worse still, to let them fail, taking an organization down with them.

There is another significant issue here. Managerial coaching is often undertaken to increase personal performance. In my coaching work over many years, I have begun to divide candidates into two groups. Leaders in the first group have drive but lack some understanding, knowledge, and/or skill. Leaders in the second group lack drive but have required knowledge and skill aplenty. Coaching success rates are high with the first group because knowledge and skill deficits can be identified, and they are teachable, so gaps can be closed. Once leaders have the required knowledge and skill, their drive ensures that they are likely to apply it even when the going gets tough.

The second group, the skilled but unwilling group, is problematic. Leaders in this group often have multiple qualifications and may have completed a wide range of skill development programs. But they are still ineffective. One chap, let's call him Brian, had four university degrees and had attended a dozen external short leadership skill development courses. At a corporate leadership program, he passed every one of the 32 competence tests with a high level of rated achievement. Six months later it was clear that Brian was still a poor performer. On the surface he looked as if he should be a high performer. He seemed to be doing everything right according to company guidelines. But the results of his unit were poor and getting worse. Only during coaching was it possible to discover why, and it's an all too familiar tale.

Despite exemplary leadership on the many occasions when it was easy, Brian was failing to act forthrightly on the few occasions when it was critical but difficult—for example, confronting poor performance, negotiating for resources for his unit, and the like. This was setting the tone for the whole unit, resulting in low morale and distrust in management. In this case, the coaching challenge was akin to instilling drive. I am confident that people can learn skill and knowledge and acquire drive if they really want to, but I have consistently found that drive is the harder of the two to train. For some it may not be trainable at all. For many it can seem to be too tough. Such people may decide that a career in management is not really what they want and seek satisfaction in another area. That is what Brian decided to do. He was successfully redeployed into a technical role and proved to be a productive contributor in that role.

What to Do About It

It is one thing to say that we can extract the desirable qualities of an exceptional personality while managing the potential risks. It is another thing to know how to do it. That is the focus of the remainder of this chapter.

PASS the Competition

I began by trying to understand my own leadership behavior and then broadened my investigation to look at the behavior of other leaders and have gradually built a systemic model of leadership effectiveness. I call this model PASS, which is an acronym for Personal Attributes, Skill, and Situation. Though the model emerged first from practical experience, I have subsequently backfilled it with solid theory. For well over a decade, the PASS model has guided my company's work in the areas of leadership development and strategy implementation (which usually depends heavily on leadership capability). Results have been positive, with many alumni reporting that involvement, while challenging, has changed not only their performance at work, but also their lives for the better. What follows is a practical summary of the PASS model.

Start Early

Most high performing supervisors and lower-level managers do not have exceptional personality characteristics. The few that do are likely to be considered mavericks or renegades. Over time it is likely that these mavericks will gravitate towards senior jobs. Managers identified early in their careers as "high potentials" are often *not* the ones who prove to be the real stars later on. All too often, the focus in early career development is on characteristics that end up not mattering much in senior roles. For example, one large multinational manufacturing organization I consulted to looked back over 20 years and found that the early-career renegades were far more effective in senior jobs than the ones who made the high potential list. Interestingly, the renegades had not done spectacularly well in junior jobs. As Lombardo and Eichinger [30] (2000) have documented, the leaders who succeed at the top tend to be learners who don't necessarily shine earlier in their careers, but accumulate insight and perspective on their steady ascent.

Lower-level job demands are not as great as senior pressure. Recent research and practice on the "leadership pipeline" illustrate how the behaviors, skills, and perspectives needed for success change as you ascend the corporate hierarchy.[4,24,25] In particular, lower-level leadership roles are less complex, concern activities that unfold over shorter time spans, have fewer constituents and stakeholders to balance, and require a narrow, technical focus.

With less demanding pressure, lower-level managers with exceptional personalities are in a prime position to begin learning about themselves and how they can better manage their strong drives. This learning can be facilitated in a leadership development process. Programs can be designed to introduce the idea of exceptional personality, to begin the introduction of relevant skill learning, and to offer on-the-job experience to embed learning behaviorally. While this is preferable, it is not always possible. Organizations do not have unlimited training budgets. Further, individuals may not be responsive to training when they do not feel a need imperative. Training seems more impactful when it is focused and "just in time."

Carol, like many others, was highly trained. But she was not lucky enough to be exposed to the right sort of development early on when her jobs were somewhat easier. Even when she attended relevant training, where I first met her, the message did not sink in enough to transfer into behavior change under pressure. She became competent but not capable. At critical times, usually when it wasn't easy, she failed to act or acted in the wrong manner. It does not take much of this for everyone to take a leader's measure. Ninety-nine percent of their behavior can be effective, but it is that one percent when it is critical that sets the tone. It wasn't until she came under great pressure, let things slide that she should not have, had no way of dealing with the difficulties she herself was creating, and ultimately feared failure, that Carol felt the need and had the motivation to do extra personal development work.

Intervening at the Top

Unfortunately, many upper-level leaders are like Carol—they didn't get an early start to honing their exceptional personalities. Most of my work has been with these individuals. The PASS development process I employ with senior leaders has many variants, but there are two common factors. First, all of the development is focused on the leadership skill set. Second, the candidate is exposed to an appropriate level of intensity.

Leadership skills. Reviews of over 100 years of leadership theory divide views of leadership into three basic domains: leader personal attributes, leader behavioral skill, and the situation faced by a leader. All three views are important, and any approach that ignores one is limited. A systemic balance of each of the three domains increases the practical impact of leadership development. I developed the PASS model as an integrative framework based on this principle (see Figure 2).

The PASS model is based on thought self-leadership.[34,35] I use needs analysis to reveal which components of the situation need to be included in the model for a particular context. The *situation* domain focuses on relationships, culture, systems dynamics, group dynamics, networks and similar concepts. Needs analysis can also reveal areas of leadership skill in which competence may be lacking in individuals, or indeed, in the culture. Three common areas are interpersonal skills, transformational skills, and communication skills. Applied skills, like conflict resolution, persuasion, selling, public speaking and the like may also be appropriate to incorporate here.

Figure 2.
The PASS model of leadership development

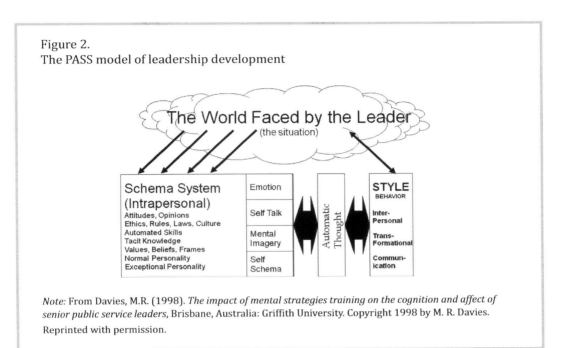

Note: From Davies, M.R. (1998). *The impact of mental strategies training on the cognition and affect of senior public service leaders*, Brisbane, Australia: Griffith University. Copyright 1998 by M. R. Davies. Reprinted with permission.

Leaders often arrive at courses listing reams of things in which they have been accredited or classes they have completed. When questioned, they often can't remember much detail. When asked to demonstrate, they often cannot or will not. So the fact that people have completed prior training may mean very little. For lower-level managers and supervisors, the situation and skill levels of training are often enough to facilitate a marked increase in their job performance. For senior managers this may not be the case. They often need more.

Development in the *personal attributes* domain is by far the most demanding for executives to undertake. Because those who I see are already senior managers, I make the assumption that everyone who goes through PASS development is already successful. They have everything they need to be even more successful, whatever success means to them in their context. I further assume that everyone self-imposes limitations of some sort. Those with drive may lack capability because of deficits in self-knowledge and skill. Those without strong drive may also lack knowledge or skill and have the additional challenge of learning drive or redefining their personal model of success. The purpose of this assessment of personal attributes is to uncover key limitations and work to overcome or redirect them.

I have tried many techniques to pinpoint personally-imposed limitations; a few seem useful but most are not. Methods that work best include guided review of objective performance, convergent interviewing of stakeholders, psychometric testing, and, with some very real limitations, 360-degree feedback. An appropriate combination of each is ideal.

Senior roles are more subjective than junior or technical roles. It becomes harder to obtain objective performance measures that are reliable and valid, if you can even get the data. For this reason creativity may be required here. Guided objective performance review is focused on specific career events, both good and bad. Common interview protocols like Behavioral Event Interviewing can be used by adding in an additional area of focus, looking for specific evidence of drive—for instance, persistence, tenacity, and/or emotional resilience beyond the norm.

One candidate we will call Joe had a stellar track record in the HR files. But Joe had been passed over twice for promotion when I spoke with him. Talking through specific episodes of his career in detail began to reveal a pattern. Joe had tenacity to burn and capability in spades, but he sometimes overdid it. He had been protected by two more senior managers who themselves had personally benefited from Joe's tenacity. But Joe had not learned the political savvy necessary in senior positions to broker competing interests of stakeholders. When the protection from above had moved on, this shortcoming became apparent. A few months of intensive coaching based on a different perspective of the organization and some behavioral development made a difference. Joe got the next promotion.

A second approach is convergent interviewing of stakeholders surrounding the role. Stakeholders may include direct reports, peers, superiors, customers, and any other people involved in significant interaction with the individual. A list of appropriate stakeholders should be identified by the focal leader. Stakeholders are then separately interviewed for approximately one hour about the focal leader's leadership. At first, interview discussions are kept general and open-ended to allow the interviewee to fully express his or her views. As the interview progresses, themes tend to emerge. Skilled questioning can be used to converge toward and tease out more detail on these themes. Repeated across a range of stakeholders, this technique often leads to significant learning about the individual that no stakeholder may have reported if asked directly.

Take the case of Susan. She reached an upper-middle level position and was set for bigger and better things. As a result she was offered the opportunity of personal coaching. Convergent interviewing revealed a negative behavioral trait excused with the oft-repeated phrase: "Oh but that's just Susan; she doesn't mean it; she's really very nice." With convergent interviewing and psychometric testing, we were able to identify a drive-related issue that could well have led to later derailment. Fortunately Susan was highly motivated and was prepared to invest effort in development. Her career has continued to progress to much higher levels, where the issues she mastered in coaching may have derailed her if left unaddressed.

A third type of assessment involves psychological testing. Psychological tests can uncover things that may not emerge easily any other way. It is important to use quality instruments that are scientifically validated and are reliable. One such tool set that I use regularly is the Leadership Forecast Series offered by Hogan Assessment Systems. This battery includes three tests: the *Hogan Personality Inventory* (a measure of bright side characteristics), the *Hogan Development Survey* (a measure of exceptional personality characteristics), and the *Motives, Values, and Preferences Inventory* (a measure of values). At the very least, data from these instruments afford individuals the opportunity of deep personal insight. This insight provides the cornerstone to development.

The idea of 360-degree feedback seems straightforward, but is not without limitations. Raters do not always simply assess behavior, but also have their own agendas. Further, 360 instruments usually give a limited number of ways that a focal individual can be scored. The relationship that raters have with the ratee may influence their ratings. When a diverse range of individuals rate a manager, it is hard, if not impossible, to account for biases that may vary across raters. Direct reports may want to send a message about something good or bad; peers may be competitors, enemies, friends, or some mixture; bosses may see the individual from a remote perspective, and so on. These reasons give me pause over 360-degree feedback. The feedback reports look precise and professional; but what if they are precisely wrong and someone's career opportunities are impacted as a result? This may be particularly problematic for driven individuals with exceptional personality characteristics that they have not yet understood and learned to manage.

Leadership development can be tailored to meet most individual and organizational needs using the above guidelines. The actual development process may involve a residential program, on-the-job work, a series of short courses, personal coaching, or any combination that fits individual needs and the demands of the environment. While it is often helpful to get people away from work for an offsite program, a series of well-designed short courses, even one evening a week over ten weeks, can improve leader capability.[7]

Development Intensity. Whatever process is used, intensity is a key aspect of the PASS training methodology and process. By intensity I refer to the emotional demand or pressure a person feels when he or she is undertaking the training. As discussed earlier in this chapter, exceptional personality characteristics are acquired through trauma. That means that patterns of behavior emerging from or related to those characteristics will be encoded in the nervous system with a level of emotional intensity. I have found that training that attempts to change or redirect those behavior patterns will not have lasting impact unless the training is intense like the original learning experience, the trauma.

Intensity introduces a serious ethical issue. It is not ethical to overwhelm people in training courses to which they have been sent. Increasing intensity means placing trainees under pressure. This must be done only with full disclosure and with informed consent from those undertaking the training. It is not ethical to expose people sent to corporate training to any more than what I subjectively define as "level six intensity." This means a subjective rating of 6 on a scale where 1 is *no intensity* (e.g., calmly relaxing) and 10 is *the most intensity imaginable* (e.g., under fire on a battlefield). Level six is a professional judgment but an important one. It is particularly unethical if the trainer is not qualified with appropriate education, training, and expertise.

Development is not therapy and should not ever attempt to be. Problem people should not be sent by their supervisors to "be fixed." Some people require more intensity than level six because the extent of their exceptional personality is so great. They may need one-on-one coaching or even a therapeutic intervention. Without an appropriate level of intensity, such individuals may be critical of the development program because it did not reach them. That is a fact of life we have to live with. Pre-interviewing and pre-surveying before acceptance into the training can minimize the problem but not eliminate it. Potential candidates with indications of high current life stressors or other turmoil should be asked to undertake preliminary work, given the opportunity to postpone until a more appropriate time, or screened out.

Concern about too much intensity aside, I believe that it is just as unethical to let those in senior positions avoid development because they might find it stressful. A lot of benefits come with senior management positions. In exchange for those benefits, incumbents have the obligation to be the best leaders they can be under the circumstances. Almost no one can claim they have nothing left to learn. It is often the people who need development most who try hardest to avoid it. HR policy and management resolve should be strong enough to ensure that people who accept the benefits of high office also meet the obligations.

Conclusion

In this chapter I have argued that leadership is a critical skill set for managers. I have referred to leadership talent as capability. Leadership capability can be based on leader personal attributes. One set of personal attributes that I have found to be particularly relevant are exceptional personality characteristics. These characteristics, which arise early in life, provide exceptional drive and focus in areas of useful functioning. The same characteristics also can be risk factors if the individuals are not self-aware and have not learned to extract the best from their drives while avoiding the worst. Some will learn how to do this from life experience. Most will benefit from developmental assistance provided that the development is carefully tailored and expertly run at an appropriate level of intensity. More than 95% of candidates I have dealt with over the last 20 years have reported that the development has made a significant difference for them. For those individuals, the learning and development led to opportunities that they would not otherwise have been able to access. This is especially so for the 20% or so who say the experience was life changing. For organizations, it has opened up a rich source of more capable leadership talent. What is needed is focus on opportunities afforded by exceptional personality and a realistic strategy for mitigating the risks.

References

1. American Psychiatric Association. (1994). *Diagnostic and statistical manual of mental disorders* (4th. ed.). Washington, DC.: Author.

2. Benson, M. J., & Campbell, J. P. (2007). To be, or not to be, linear: An expanded representation of personality and its relationship to leadership performance. *International Journal of Selection and Assessment, 15*, 232-249.

3. Board, B. J. & Fritzon, K. F. (2005). Disordered personalities at work. *Psychology, Crime, and Law, 11*, 17-32.

4. Charan, R., Drotter, S., & Noel, J. (2001). *The leadership pipeline: How to build the leadership-powered company*. San Francisco: Jossey-Bass.

5. Collins, J. (2001). *Good to great*. New York: HarperBusiness.

6. Collins, J. (2003, July 21). The 10 greatest CEOs of all time. *Fortune*, 54-68.

7. Davies, M. R. (1998). *The impact of mental strategies training on the cognition and affect of senior public service leaders*. Brisbane, Australia: Griffith University.

8. Davies, M. R. (2005). *Prediction of transformational leadership by personality constructs for senior Australian organizational executive leaders*. Unpublished doctoral dissertation, Griffith University, Brisbane, Australia.

9. Gardner, H. (1995). *Leading minds: An anatomy of leadership*. New York: Basic Books.

10. Gentry, W. A., & Chappellow, C. T. (this volume). Managerial derailment: Weaknesses that can be fixed.

11. Hall, L. M., Bodenhamer, B. G., Bolstad, R., & Hamblett, M. (2001). *The structure of personality: Modeling "Personality" using NLP and Neuro-Semantics*. Bancyfelin, Wales: Crown House Publishing Limited.

12. Hambrick, D. C., Finkelstein, S., & Mooney, A. (2005). Executive job demands: New insights for explaining strategic decisions and leader behaviors. *Academy of Management Review, 30*, 472–491.

13. Hofstede, G. (1991). *Cultures and organizations: Intercultural cooperation and its importance for survival*. London: HarperCollins.

14. Hogan, R. (2006a). *Personality and the fate of organizations*. Mahwah, NJ: Lawrence Erlbaum Associates., Inc.

15. Hogan, R. (2006b). *The TEC CEO leadership study. Sydney: A joint research project between The Executive Connection, Hogan Assessment Systems, and Peter Berry Consultancy*. Tulsa, OK.: Hogan Assessment Systems.

16. Hogan, R., & Benson, M. J. (this volume). Personality theory and positive psychology: Strategic self-awareness.

17. Hogan, R., Curphy, G. J., & Hogan, J. (1994). What we know about leadership: Effectiveness and personality. *American Psychologist, 49*(6), 493-504.

18. Hogan, R., & Hogan, J. (1997). *Hogan Development Survey Manual*. Tulsa, OK.: Hogan Assessment Systems.

19. Hogan, R., & Hogan, J. (2001). Assessing leadership: A view of the dark side. *International Journal of Selection and Assessment, 9*, 40-51.

20. Hogan, R., & Kaiser, R. B. (2005). What we know about leadership. *Review of General Psychology*, *9*(2), 169-180.

21. Hogan, R., Hogan, J., & Warrenfelz, R. (2007). *The Hogan guide: Interpretation and Use of Hogan Inventories*. Tulsa, OK: Hogan Assessment Systems.

22. Horney, K. (1950). *Neurosis and human growth: The struggle toward self-realization.* New York: W. W. Norton & Company, Inc.

23. Judge, T. A., Bono, J. E., Ilies, R., & Gerhardt, M. W. (2002). Personality and leadership: A qualitative and quantitative review. *Journal of Applied Psychology*, *87*, 765-780.

24. Kaiser, R. B. (2005). *Filling the leadership pipeline.* Greensboro, NC: Center for Creative Leadership.

25. Kaiser, R. B., & Craig, S. B. (2004, April). What gets you there won't keep you there: Managerial behaviors related to effectiveness at the bottom, middle, and top. In R. B. Kaiser & S. B. Craig (Co-chairs), *Filling the pipe I: Studying management development across the hierarchy.* Symposium presented at the 19th Annual Conference of the Society for Industrial and Organizational Psychology, Chicago, IL.

26. Kaiser, R. B., & Kaplan, R. E. (this volume). When strengths run amok.

27. Kaiser, R. B., Hogan, R., & Craig, S. B. (2008). Leadership and the fate of organizations. *American Psychologist*, *63*, 96-110.

28. Lenzenweger, M. F., & Clarkin, J. F. (1996). The personality disorders: History, classification, and research issues. In J. F. Clarkin & M. F. Lenzenweger (Eds.), *Major theories of personality disorder* (pp. 1-35). New York: Guilford Press.

29. Levinson, H. (1988). You won't recognize me: Predictions about changes in top management characteristics. *The Academy of Management Executive*, *11*(2), 119-125.

30. Lombardo, M., & Eichinger, R. (2000). High potentials as high learners. *Human Resource Management*, *39*, 321-329.

31. Macoby, M. (2000). Narcissistic leaders: The incredible pros, the inevitable cons. *Harvard Business Review*, *78*(1), 69-77.

32. McCall, M. W., Jr. (this volume). Every strength a weakness and other caveats.

33. Miller, D. (1990). *The Icarus paradox: How exceptional companies bring about their own downfall.* New York: HarperBusiness.

34. Neck, C. P. (1992). *Thought self-leadership: The impact of mental strategies training on employee cognition, behaviors, and emotions.* Unpublished doctoral dissertation, Arizona State University, Tempe, Arizona.

35. Neck, C. P., & Manz, C. C. (1996). Thought self-leadership: The impact of mental strategies training on employee cognition, behavior, and affect. *Journal of Organizational Behavior*, *17*, 445-467.

SECTION 4

Conclusion

CHAPTER 10

STRENTHS-BASED DEVELOPMENT IN PERSPECTIVE

Randall P. White, Ph.D.
Executive Development Group and Duke Corporate Education

Marcus Buckingham, a leading advocate of the strengths movement, is one of the best examples of why the "stick with your strengths" strategy doesn't work. In a television interview on the April 20, 2007 episode of the *Today Show*, an NBC reporter said that Buckingham had overcome "his own weakness to reach the top of the guru game. As a child, he stuttered. Years later his speech, once his weakness, is now his greatest strength."

In my almost 30 years of experience studying executives and what makes good ones great, I have never been struck as sharply as I was by the irony of the previous statement. Buckingham was talking from the road on his city-to-city bus tour, talking to companies and schools about going with your strengths and leaving the rest behind. Yet his own professional beginnings illustrate a behavior counter to his current message. A characteristic of all great leaders is the ability to learn, grow, and adapt—to overcome weaknesses and develop new strengths to fit a changing world. And as the collection of chapters in this book makes clear, only the self-aware, not the strong, survive.

In this concluding chapter, I take stock of the previous chapters and offer my own point of view on strengths-based development. By building on the contributions of nine authorship teams along with my own direct experience as both a student of leadership and a teacher of leaders, I try to put the strengths-based approach to development in perspective. In a nutshell, I believe that the seductive appeal of the strengths movement obscures how this philosophy inhibits learning, growth, and adaptability—the leading indicators of success in an ever-shifting, dynamic, and hypercompetitive global marketplace.

Ready for a Simple Solution

Having gotten to this point in the book, you have run the gauntlet of reasons why an exclusive focus on strengths is shortsighted. My colleagues have all taken great pains to point out why a strengths-based approach, when examined in the cold light of day, is not up to the challenge of producing the skilled, dynamic, and adaptable leaders required to succeed in today's turbulent economy.

Right now the American ethos is primed for finding a quick fix. The economy stinks. We're in a leadership crisis. We're looking for answers. In the work place, people constantly bend and flex in new directions—a response to changing technologies, merging businesses, stiff competition, and an uncertain economy. We're seeking relief. So when a new movement—like the strengths movement—comes along promising easy answers, it gets the rock-star treatment: the bus across America, the Oprah interview.

Permission to Stagnate

For the moment proponents of the strengths movement seem to be passing out permission slips: "Stop stretching yourself in so many different directions. Focus instead on what you can do, not what you can't." Once the tour bus packs up and heads for another city, reality sinks in. It doesn't matter how hard you wave that permission slip. The nature of business requires that you shed the strengths you no longer need, and develop the new ones required to remain viable and relevant.

The danger comes with looking toward any one single solution as a savior. And as my colleagues have shown here, relying on our strengths is the antithesis of what we need. Research and experience shows that in times like these, we need something different. Something we've never done before. In total, the chapters in this book make a compelling case for why the strengths movement simply isn't strong enough for the modern workplace. Continuous learning and dealing with the unknown is critical to development and continued success.[6,8,18]

Whither Growth and Development?

Relying too heavily on one's strengths is a key dynamic leading to executive derailment because it promotes stasis and stagnation while inhibiting growth and development.[17,20,3] The danger in yoking our future to what worked in the past is multiplied by the fact that many of today's executives don't know what their company truly needs from its leaders to win in the global marketplace.

Further complicating matters are the complex issues skirted over by simple admonishments to "play to your strengths." In chapter four, McCall[15] explained how it is tenuous to define a strength as a strength, given the contextual nature of leadership—a strength in one environment (for instance, a no-nonsense approach to cost cutting in a mature market with eroding margins) isn't necessarily a strength in another (a start-up venture selling a new product in an emerging market). Elaborating on this theme in chapter five, Kaiser and Kaplan[11] showed how leaders routinely flex the wrong strengths—not knowing their strengths, they are prone to applying them at the wrong time and to the wrong degree, and this comes at the expense of complementary skills that also have their time and place.

In my own research[6] and in that of my colleagues,[14,18] we have found that continuous learning and dealing with the unknown, untested, and untried may be the secret to success. But this is undermined by playing to an individual's strengths. Exploiting one's strengths by repeatedly assigning the person to one type of job (for instance, a "fix-it" person for turnaround situations) robs the individual of the opportunity to develop a wider repertoire and broader perspective, which will matter at the top. Playing to strengths may have a short-term advantage—you capitalize on deep smarts and well-honed skills—but this strategy also has a long-term disadvantage: the opportunity cost in not providing the diversity of job experiences needed to develop a seasoned and well-rounded leader for the future.

Trends in areas as distinct as executive turnover and evolutionary neuroscience highlight the centrality of learning to sustainable success. The short-lived tenure of today's chief executive—somewhere in the neighborhood of two years, on average—and the plasticity of the brain converge to underscore how learning is critical not just for your career but for survival itself.[4] On the October 21, 2007 episode of *Meet the Press*, the political biographer Doris Kearns Goodwin stated that the best candidate for president of the United States would be the one who could learn, grow, and change—hardly the poster child for finding your strengths and building a career around them.

The development of effective leaders involves transitioning through a series of increasingly difficult and complex skills. This is an interesting set of ideas first put forth by Elliott Jaques, who argued that increases in organizational complexity demand a greater ability to imagine further into the future (for a practical elaboration of this notion, see Jacque's 1989 book, *Requisite Organization*). Hence, as a leader deals with greater complexity at each stage in his or her career, he or she needs to be armed with a more widely developed skill set and a broader perspective for viewing complex problems and anticipating the consequences of various solutions.

Thinly Veiled Self-Indulgence

There is an insidious reason why the strengths-based approach may resonate with individuals, especially in cultures that embrace Western individualism. By giving out permission slips to ignore weaknesses, the strengths-based approach excuses individual leaders from the hard work of development. In effect, it says: "Those mean managers, they want you to be something you are not. They are telling you to fix your weakness in math and working with numbers and financial reports. They don't recognize that you are an artist; instead of giving you a hard time about math, they should give you paint, brushes, and a canvas." But what if the person's job is an accounting manager?

When expressed with a single-minded focus, the strengths movement is an exercise in self-indulgence. It focuses on what comes easy for the individual, what the individual enjoys doing, and what will bring the individual fulfillment. What is ignored in this philosophy is what the organization needs from the position that the individual's job is designed to provide. As Rob Kaiser has said, "Leadership roles are not elective—if the leader cannot effectively fill those roles, the performance of the team and organization will inevitably suffer."[10] The philosophy behind the strengths approach offers yet another example of putting the needs of the individual above the needs of the greater good.

A Single-minded Focus on Strengths Can't Work

Out of the Comfort Zone

In chapter two, Bob Eichinger, Guangrong Dai, and KingYii Tang[2] restated a question from two grown children entering the world of work: "Would a strengths-based approach be the best way to manage my career?" I can't imagine a parent saying to a child, "Stick with what you know, kid—you probably won't get any better." I wouldn't say that to a child, nor would I say it to a leader.

For the sake of the argument, Eichinger, Dai, and Tang took on a strengths-based strategy and assumed it to be true. With this assumption in mind, they did an analysis of the most successful mangers. What they found is that the more you hone those strengths to be successful—the skills in short supply that matter most to effective leadership—the closer you move to a smaller group of people, competing at your level, who have exactly the same strengths as you. And if you're among the top 10% of the people Eichinger and his colleagues studied, the competition is fierce. Everybody looks the same. The range is restricted. To stand out, you've got to be willing to learn what you—and they—can't do, or don't know how to do. To differentiate, you've got to strengthen your current strengths as well as develop new ones.

The point is we don't tell children, "Stick with the crayons, kid. You'll never get better with anything else." We encourage them to try a variety of things. The same is true for leaders: the great ones discover what they didn't even know they could do.

Flexing the Wrong Strengths

In chapter three, Jean Brittain Leslie and Anand Chandrasekar[13] of the Center for Creative Leadership point out a disconnect between what leaders are good at and what organizations need them to be good at. Most executives have their greatest strengths in areas that aren't central to the kind of dynamic leadership organizations need to be competitive. The danger these executives could face is relying on strengths that won't make them a better leader. Leslie and Chandrasekar wrote:

> "The skills most prevalent among managers—that is, their current strengths—are not the same as the skills that are most critical to organizational performance. If we're going to tell managers to rely on their strengths, there's good cause for concern that they would be applying the wrong skills."

Development is Hard Work

Finding flaws is human. Growth and development—especially in areas in which one is weak, or even flawed—takes humility and hard work, not to mention rising above one's ego. Right down to the core of the human psyche, it's actually easier to believe in a notion of a perfect leader than it is to do the work necessary to change and become a better or more effective leader.

In chapter four, Morgan McCall[15] suggested that we think too highly of ourselves—mostly around skills that don't matter. As if an answer to the unspoken prayer, the recent emphasis on playing people to their strengths provides just such an escape. There's an underlying belief that talent is born not made, and if you just aren't born with a natural inclination in a particular area, well, just forget it. We all know that's not true.

As one extraordinary French executive said, "To me, the real test of leadership is getting people to follow you and do something, even when they don't have to," suggesting that leadership isn't about just being great at something, it's about inspiring other people to greatness.

Global Leadership and Shifting Standards

McCall and George Hollenbeck, in a 2002 study of global executives living and working in foreign cultures, found that what was a strength in one culture could become a decided disadvantage while transitioning into a different one. Global leadership requires that you change and adapt to fit the customs and the cultures of the country you're in. "What worked splendidly in one culture could bring disaster in the next. Global transitions required reassessing, sometimes letting go, sometimes adding to, sometimes both, but rarely staying the course," they said.[16]

Save Yourself from Your Strengths

In the original "derailment" studies at the Center for Creative Leadership, it was discovered that the "jack of all trades," not the strongest, survived (see the review of this research in chapter seven, by Bill Gentry and Craig Chappelow).[3] In fact, McCall and Lombardo's[17] original study found the secret to long-term career success is having a well-rounded portfolio of skills and a lack of glaring weaknesses. Successful executives learned a little bit of everything. Derailed managers, on the other hand, relied too much on a few towering strengths to the neglect of complementary skill sets. This prompted McCall and Lombardo to declare a now well-known phrase: "strengths can become weaknesses." Later research demonstrated that managers who derail in the middle of their careers can turn it around and get back on track if they were willing to make an honest self-appraisal of both their strengths and weaknesses.[12]

Batter up

Playing to your strengths is only as good as the degree of certainty and stability in your situation. In chapter eight, Robert Hogan and Michael Benson[7] used a baseball analogy. Fielding a baseball team, the person chosen to play short-stop needs specific strengths because he'll always be in that position. Same thing for pitchers, catchers, outfielders, and the rest of the infield because their positions too are well defined.

Yet business is certainly uncertain. In his classic 1975 *Harvard Business Review* article, "The Manager's Job: Folklore and Fact," Henry Mintzberg showed the range of unpredictable events executives have to field each day. Several studies have confirmed Mintzberg's original finding that managers work at an "unrelenting pace, that their activities are characterized by brevity, variety, and discontinuity, and that they are strongly oriented to action, and dislike reflective activities."

Dealing with this uncertainty makes leaders great. Successful leadership in such an environment is born from unpredictability, mistakes and "redos," and the individual's openness to accept challenges. In our research we found that managers who can tolerate risk also value the learning opportunity afforded by making mistakes.[6] In fact, one executive we consulted to said that he wants his employees to fail fast, but to fail forward.

The greatest risk in not trying new things is overplaying what you know—a proven cause of derailment. This is a line extension to the natural development process. Skills in childhood won't serve adolescence. And a young adult can't rely on the skills that got him through his teens to serve him in adulthood. What is more off-putting and frustrating than a middle-aged man acting like a young man in a hurry with something to prove?

The Seductive Appeal of the Strengths Movement

A collective sigh of relief could have been heard in cubicles and boardrooms across the Western world when company leaders first embraced "the new thing" in leadership development—the strengths movement. The modern workplace today is an anxious one. Leadership trends and project plans rarely survive the fiscal year. In the course of a day, people flex and bend outside their comfort zones as technology comes and goes, businesses merge, fold, or struggle to break even. One result is a lackluster love affair with leadership.

The United States is an ideal environment for the strengths movement. It's built into the American ethos to find a strength and build on it. If a little is good, a lot must be better. Go to McDonald's and you'll pay the lowest price for the biggest burger, a Big Mac loaded with 485 calories and 21.5 grams of fat—it even tastes good, while slowly it is making you sick.

Even if we don't necessarily know what they are, the reality is that we all have strengths and weaknesses. As Americans, we have a uniquely inflated sense of abilities in general. In my teaching around the world, I find that 80% of people in the United States lean heavily towards using fours and fives (on a five-point scale) in their ratings of others and themselves. In the classes I've taught in Germany and particularly in Scandinavia, people rarely think in fives—they think in threes. Yet in the U. S., we have a cultural halo around everyone's head. We don't use *C*s. We don't differentiate. Everyone is an *A* or *B*—think Garrison Keillor's Lake Wobegon, "where all the children are above average."

The Successful Don't Rest on their Strengths

My own work with leaders suggests that the most effective ones are able to embrace uncertainty where a pattern set of leadership behaviors may not be useful.[6] If this is true for individuals, it's even more true for a collection of individuals—an organization. Organizations continually demonstrate that going outside their strengths is key to survival and greater success. I recently came across two companies, two leaders in the global leadership landscape who embraced what they didn't know as a deliberate leadership strategy.

Charting Terra Nova

In 2007 many newspaper organizations either braced for or announced company layoffs. One Norwegian media company, Schibsted, reported that its earnings rose 28% in the fourth quarter. Online operations will generate about 20% of the company's revenue this year. Meanwhile, many traditional news businesses are struggling or folding.[21]

Schibsted's success actually started in 1995 when the global newspaper industry faced a fateful decision: Go with new digital media or stay with old print media. As other organizations hesitated, Schibsted invested heavily in new media, building credibility and the content of their online newspapers. They started charging for advertising space—and let the readers read for free.

In 2000 and 2001, Schibsted didn't bail out when they could have because they continued to believe in the unknown—the unforeseen potential of online media. Leaders in the company said they recognized early that the Internet would change the traditional print industry. They hired experts from outside the newspaper industry to assist in the reinvention. They abandoned what made them successful in the print world and boldly embraced what the company (and the whole industry, for that matter) had never done before.

Using Strengths to Find Weakness

While Google has grown by acquiring new businesses, the acquisition process has created a unique weakness. As businesses merge with Google, they bring a new set of people, organizational processes, and cultural mindsets. The result has been a patchwork of sewn-together, fast-fix solutions for sales and business processes.[5]

In January 2008, the Internet analysis group Comscore released its findings on the number of people who clicked on Google's paid ads. On its Web site, Comscore reported a 33% decline in the number of people who clicked through Google's paid advertising links in 2007.[22] With the struggle to sell ads on YouTube, coupled with complaints from salespeople about a slow, paper-heavy process of purchasing ads, Google launched a hands-on fact-finding mission.

In March 2008, Tim Armstrong, Google's head of advertising and commerce in North America, moved himself from his executive office into the middle of the YouTube ad team's cubicle spaces. Determined, he said, to figure out the sales process, he emerged a month later with a list of 105 problems to be fixed. The company has a history of similar initiatives designed to clear the clutter and do the dirty work, including, "Project Spaghetti," "Weed Days," and "Project Drano."

Google's billions in annual sales would have caused celebration in any other company. Yet Google didn't rely on the strength of past or predicted sales revenues to improve business. They literally did a deep-dive to seek and find problems. They spotted a weakness and jumped right into the middle of it. With this strategy, Google seemed to be following the insights of Hogan and Benson, who described in chapter eight how there is no news in good news and that "performance only improves if people know what they are doing wrong."

As of the writing of this book, the jury is still out about Google and whether the company will be a long-term success story or not. Nonetheless, the actions of several leaders at the company underscore the need to move away from simply building on strengths to also examining the downsides, the negatives, and the "fix-its." Whether or not Google is a success in the long run is beyond the point: The willingness to be reflective, and examine their weaknesses, and not just assume they'll go away, is the critical point. Google is willing to look at its weaknesses and not be blinded by its strengths.

The Situation Comedy of Executive Education?

A strength can become formulaic, predictable with tidy conclusions—like a situation comedy. The formula works, proves successful, and is repeated again and again. You get the same variety of roles, and you put people in the same roles again and again. Soon the audience becomes numb. There is no difference, no variety. It's the same episode repeated over and over. And in chapter six, Steven Berglas[1] offered the fallen CEO and founder of Digital Equipment Corporation, Ken Olsen, as a cautionary tale about what happens when leaders rely on the same old tricks.

Remember when you first saw John Cleese and the rest of the cast of *Monty Python's Flying Circus*? It was a troop of actors trying new and different things. Were they playing to their strengths? Or were they celebrating absurdity? Their formula was to be imperfect and to be in the moment—leverage their strengths absolutely, but also stretch themselves into risky new territories and, ultimately, allow themselves to learn and grow.

If we only play to our strengths, will we ever learn to laugh at ourselves for trying? To only play to our strengths means we will stop growing—and that is surely not a laughing matter.

References

1. Berglas, S. (this volume). Victims of their own success.

2. Eichinger, R. W., Dai, G., & Tang, K. Y. (this volume). It depends upon what you mean by a strength.

3. Gentry, W. A. & Chappelow, C. T. (this volume). Managerial derailment: Weaknesses that can be fixed.

4. Gilkey, R. & Kilts, C. (2007). Cognitive fitness, *Harvard Business Review*, *85*(11), 53-66.

5. Google push to sell ads on YouTube hits snags. (2008, July 9). *Wall Street Journal,* p, A1.

6. Hodgson, P., & White, R. P. (2001). *Relax, it's only uncertainty.* London: Prentice Hall.

7. Hogan, R., & Benson, M. J. (this volume). Personality theory and positive psychology: Strategic self-awareness.

8. Hogan, R., & Warrenfeltz, R. (2003). Educating the modern manager. *Academy of Management Learning and Education, 2*, 74-84.

9. Jaques, E. (1989). *Requisite organization: The CEO's guide to creative structure and leadership*. Arlington, VA: Cason Hall.

10. Kaiser, R. B. (2007, April). *The perils of accentuating the positives*. Symposium presented at the 22nd Annual Conference of the Society for Industrial and Organizational Psychology, New York, NY.

11. Kaiser, R. B., & Kaplan, R. E. (this volume). When strengths run amok.

12. Kovach, B. E. (1989). Successful derailment: What fast-trackers can learn while they're off the track. *Organizational Dynamics, 18*(2), 33-47.

13. Leslie, J. B., & Chandrasekar, A. (this volume). Managerial strengths and organizational needs: A crucial leadership gap.

14. Lombardo M. M., & Eichinger, R. W. (2006). *The leadership machine: Architecture to develop leaders for any future* (3rd ed.). Minneapolis, MN: Lominger Limited, Inc.

15. McCall, M. W., Jr. (this volume). Every strength a weakness and other caveats.

16. McCall, M. W., Jr., & Hollenbeck, G. P. (2002). *Developing global executives.* Boston: Harvard Business School Press.

17. McCall, M. W., Jr., & Lombardo, M. M. (1983). *Off the track: Why and how successful executives get derailed.* Greensboro, NC: Center for Creative Leadership.

18. McCall, M. W., Jr., Lombardo, M. M., & Morrison, A. M. (1988). *Lessons of experience: How successful executives develop on the job.* New York: Free Press.

19. Mintzberg, H. (1975). The manager's job: Folklore and fact. *Harvard Business Review, 53*, 100-110.

20. Morrison, A. M., White, R. P., & Van Velsor, E. (1987). *Breaking the glass ceiling: Can women reach the top of America's largest corporations?* Reading, MA: Addison-Wesley.

21. While others struggle. (2007, February 19). *New York Times*, p. C2.

22. Why Google's surprising paid click data are less surprising. (2008, February 29). Online document retrieved February 29, 2008 from: http://www.comscore.com/blog/2008/02/why_googles_surprising_paid_click_data_are_less_surprising.html.